LIVING THROUGH THE COLD WAR

LIVING
UNDER THE THREAT OF
NUCLEAR WAR

Edited by Derek C. Maus

Bruce Glassman, *Vice President*
Bonnie Szumski, *Publisher*
Helen Cothran, *Managing Editor*
Scott Barbour, *Series Editor*

GREENHAVEN PRESS
An imprint of Thomson Gale, a part of The Thomson Corporation

Detroit • New York • San Francisco • San Diego • New Haven, Conn.
Waterville, Maine • London • Munich

LIBRARY OF CONGRESS CATALOGING-IN-PUBLICATION DATA

Living under the threat of nuclear war / Derek C. Maus, book editor.
    p. cm. — (Living through the Cold War)
  Includes bibliographical references and index.
  ISBN 0-7377-2130-8 (lib. : alk. paper)
    1. Nuclear weapons—History—20th century—Sources. 2. Cold War—Sources.
I. Maus, Derek C. II. Series.

U264.L578 2005
355.02'17—dc22
                                                2003067535

CONTENTS

Chapter 1: The Leaders Speak on Nuclear Weapons

Chapter 2: Cultural Aspects of the Nuclear Threat

Chapter 3: Voices of Protest

At the midpoint of the Cold War, in early 1968, U.S. television viewers saw surprising reports from Vietnam, where American ground troops had been fighting since 1965. They learned that South Vietnamese Communist rebels, known as the Vietcong, had attacked unexpectedly throughout the country. At one point Vietcong insurgents engaged U.S. troops and officials in a firefight at the very center of U.S. power in Vietnam, the American embassy in South Vietnam's capital, Saigon. Meanwhile, thousands of soldiers and marines faced a concerted siege at Khe Sanh, an isolated base high in central Vietnam's mountains. Their adversary was not the Vietcong, but rather the regular North Vietnamese army.

Reporters and U.S. citizens quickly learned that these events constituted the Tet Offensive, a coordinated attack by Vietnamese Communists that occurred in late January, the period of Tet, Vietnam's new year. The American public was surprised by the Tet Offensive because they had been led to believe that the United States and its South Vietnamese allies were winning the war, that Vietcong forces were weak and dwindling, and that the massive buildup of American forces (there were some five hundred thousand U.S. troops in Vietnam by early 1968), ensured that the south would remain free of a Communist takeover. Since 1965, politicians, pundits, and generals had claimed that massive American intervention was justified and that the war was being won. On a publicity tour in November 1967 General William Westmoreland, the American commander in Vietnam, had assured officials and reporters that "the ranks of the Vietcong are thinning steadily" and that "we have reached a point where the end begins to come into view." President Lyndon B. Johnson's advisers, meanwhile, continually encouraged him to publicly emphasize "the light at the end of the tunnel."

Ordinary Americans had largely supported the troop build-up in Vietnam, believing the argument that the country was an important front in the Cold War, the global effort to stop the spread of communism that had begun in the late 1940s. Communist regimes already held power in nearby China, North Korea, and in northern Vietnam; it was deemed necessary to hold the line in the south not only to prevent communism from taking hold there but to prevent other nations from falling to communism throughout Asia. In 1965, polls showed that 80 percent of Americans believed that intervention in Vietnam was justified despite the fact that involvement in this fight would alter American life in numerous ways. For example, young men faced the possibility of being drafted and sent to fight—and possibly die—in a war thousands of miles away. As the war progressed, citizens watched more and more of their sons—both draftees and enlisted men—being returned to the United States in coffins (approximately fifty-eight thousand Americans died in Vietnam). Antiwar protests roiled college campuses and sometimes the streets of major cities. The material costs of the war threatened domestic political reforms and America's economic health, offering the continuing specter of rising taxes and shrinking services. Nevertheless, as long as the fight was succeeding, a majority of Americans could accept these risks and sacrifices.

Tet changed many minds, suggesting as it did that the war was not, in fact, going well. When CBS news anchor Walter Cronkite, who was known as "the most trusted man in America," suggested in his broadcast on the evening of February 27 that the Vietnam War might be unwinnable and could only end in a stalemate, many people wondered if he might be right and began to suspect that the positive reports from generals and politicians might have been misleading. It was a turning point in the battle for public opinion. Johnson reportedly said that Cronkite's expressions of doubt signaled the loss of mainstream America's support for the war. Indeed, after Tet more and more people joined Cronkite in wondering whether fighting this obscure enemy in an isolated country halfway around the world was worth the cost—whether it was a truly important front in the Cold War. They made their views known through demonstrations and opinion polls, and politicians were forced to respond. In a dramatic and unexpected turn of events, Johnson declined to run for reelection in 1968, stating that his involvement in the political campaign would detract from his efforts to negotiate a peace agreement with North Vietnam. His successor, Richard Nixon, won the election after promising to end the war.

The Tet Offensive and its consequences provide strong examples of how the Cold War touched the lives of ordinary Americans. Far from being an abstract geopolitical event, the Cold War, as Tet reveals, was an ever-present influence in the everyday life of the nation. Greenhaven Press's Living Through the Cold War series provides snapshots into the lives of ordinary people during the Cold War, as well as their reactions to its major events and developments. Each volume is organized around a particular event or distinct stage of the Cold War. Primary documents such as eyewitness accounts and speeches give firsthand insights into both ordinary peoples' experiences and leaders' decisions. Secondary sources provide factual information and place events within a larger global and historical context. Additional resources include a detailed introduction, a comprehensive chronology, and a thorough bibliography. Also included are an annotated table of contents and a detailed index to help the reader locate information quickly. With these features, the Living Through the Cold War series reveals the human dimension of the superpower rivalry that defined the globe during most of the latter half of the twentieth century.

▥ INTRODUCTION

The long period of hostility between the United States and the Soviet Union that started in the aftermath of World War II is most frequently referred to as the Cold War. Another term often applied to this time period is the Atomic Age, although this refers to the years after 1942, when physicist Enrico Fermi created the first controlled atomic chain reaction. For the purposes of this book, however, the most apt name for the years 1945 through 1991 comes from the celebrated American poet W.H. Auden, who published a book in 1947 under the title *The Age of Anxiety*. The development of atomic weapons at the close of World War II had two immediate effects: It helped hasten Japan's surrender (although the extent to which it did so has been the subject of considerable debate among historians), and it created a new kind of threat that the world had never encountered before. By 1960, a mere fifteen years after the first bomb was built, the United States and the Soviet Union each possessed enough nuclear weapons to make the planet uninhabitable. For the first time in history, humans had the ability to obliterate themselves entirely from existence. Given this state of affairs and the reaction it caused, Auden's name for the period is perhaps the most appropriate, since it emphasizes the psychological distress that living with the constant threat of destruction can cause.

How the Anxiety Began

Even before the United States dropped atomic bombs on the Japanese cities of Hiroshima and Nagasaki in August 1945, World War II had been more violent than any previous human conflict. Not only had the actual fighting claimed more lives than all the wars of the nineteenth and twentieth centuries combined, but World War II had introduced a number of new horrors. For example, Germany had begun the practice of

9

deliberately bombing civilian targets when it attacked British cities in 1941 and 1942 during what came to be known as "the Blitz." Allied bombers would later adopt similar tactics. In fact, their firebombings of the German city of Dresden and the Japanese capital of Tokyo claimed the lives of hundreds of thousands of civilians almost overnight. In addition, the Nazi system of concentration camps was revealed to the world in the final stages of the war, and it quickly became clear that these had been part of a campaign of mass murder on a previously unimaginable scale. Historians have generally estimated that these camps claimed more than 6 million lives. In short, World War II had been a conflict so destructive that it truly seemed to embody the title that had once been given to World War I: "the war to end all wars."

The establishment of the United Nations in 1945 seemed to offer a ray of hope that the nations of the world could come together to find a way to resolve their future conflicts peacefully. Unfortunately, the reemergence of the ideological differences that had been laid aside during the war in order to focus on the common enemy of fascist Germany took place not long after the end of the fighting. Even before the end of the war, both nations had already begun planning ways to shape the postwar world according to their own doctrines. For example, Soviet premier Joseph Stalin intentionally ordered his Red Army troops to move as quickly as possible to occupy areas in Eastern and Central Europe that had been liberated from the retreating German forces. In doing so, he hoped both to build up goodwill toward the Soviets and, more importantly, to establish enough control over these areas to maintain an influence over them after the end of the war. His policy was largely successful, as most of the nations of Eastern Europe became Communist-dominated "client" states soon after 1945.

On the other hand, Harry Truman, who had become president when Franklin Roosevelt died in April 1945, strongly distrusted Stalin and looked for nearly every opportunity to limit any potential gains the Soviets could make as the war wound down. In fact, some revisionist historians—Gar Alperovitz most prominent among them—have claimed that Truman

used the atomic bombs against Japan not only to accelerate the end of the war but also to send a message to Stalin not to make any effort to extend his influence in Asia. Historian Margot Henriksen sums up the main point of *Atomic Diplomacy*, Alperovitz's controversial study of early atomic history, as follows:

> The United States wanted to dominate the Soviet Union during the peace [after World War II], and the bomb was the instrument of choice: it would intimidate the Soviets and it would particularly reduce their role in Asia once the war had ended without their deep involvement— which the bomb could ensure. Alperovitz noted that American officials believed that the Pacific war could be concluded by a Soviet declaration of war against Japan,

a modification of the surrender terms . . . or a combination of the two. The war was almost over, no invasion was seen as needed, yet the atomic bombs were dropped on Hiroshima and Nagasaki.[1]

The notion that Truman was using the atomic bomb to intimidate the Soviet Union into acting according to his will was reinforced when a pair of atomic bombs were tested for an audience that included invited Soviet officials in July 1946 near the Bikini atoll in the South Pacific. Less than a year later, Truman announced what came to be known as the Truman Doctrine, a policy stating that the United States had a duty "to support free peoples who are resisting subjugation by armed minorities or by outside pressures." Truman intended this statement as a clear threat—one backed up with the atomic bomb—to fight Stalin's efforts at expanding Soviet influence. As a result, many historians date the Cold War back to this "declaration" by Truman.

The Atomic Club Expands Its Membership

At the time Truman issued his doctrine, the United States was still the only country to have successfully developed a nuclear bomb. Furthermore, American intelligence experts estimated that the Soviets were at least five to ten years away from achieving their own nuclear weapons. However, the Soviet Union had begun a secret development program of its own during World War II and, through a combination of innovative scientific thinking and extensive espionage, was moving closer to testing a bomb of its own at a much faster rate than predicted. When evidence of a Soviet bomb test was discovered in September 1949, the chilling reality that the U.S. nuclear monopoly had ended quickly set in. Historian Paul Boyer writes:

The dominant reaction [to the Soviet test] was a grim determination to increase America's lead in nuclear weaponry. The Russian bomb accelerated the shift toward viewing the atomic bomb not as a terrible scourge to be eliminated as quickly as possible, but a winning weapon to be stockpiled with utmost urgency.[2]

Making sure that the atomic bomb remained a "winning weapon" meant not only increasing the number of bombs but also increasing their power.

The greatest increase in the power of nuclear weapons—and the first great period of atomic anxiety—came as a result of the development of the hydrogen bomb. Both the United States and the Soviet Union tested hydrogen bombs in the early 1950s that were hundreds of times more powerful than the bombs that had been dropped on Hiroshima and Nagasaki. These "superbombs" not only made it possible to destroy a huge city like Moscow or New York with only one bomb but also brought the issue of radioactive fallout to the forefront, since they produced massive amounts of toxic ash and dust that would present a lingering danger not only to survivors of the actual blast but to others up to hundreds of miles away. Journalists Stephen Hilgartner, Richard C. Bell, and Rory O'Connor note the effect the fallout from a particular hydrogen bomb test in 1954 had on public opinion:

> Fallout became an international public-relations problem that the AEC [Atomic Energy Commission, the U.S. government agency in charge of nuclear weapons] was never again able to quiet after the March 1, 1954, *BRAVO* test. This 15-megaton hydrogen-bomb explosion produced lethal levels of fallout over a 7,000 square-mile area of the Pacific, killing a Japanese crewman on the fishing boat *Lucky Dragon* and heavily contaminating a group of American personnel and Marshall Islanders.[3]

Growing public awareness of the nature of atomic weapons coincided with the localized but intense fighting of the Korean War (1950–1953), in which Russian and Chinese-backed North Korean troops fought against a combination of troops from South Korea, the United States, and the United Nations. This precarious situation—made worse by the occasional pleas by some military and political leaders to consider the use of atomic weapons against North Korea—ensured that the unique anxieties of life in the Atomic Age began to hit home widely for the first time.

Governmental Attempts to Control the Anxiety

A steady stream of grim predictions and vivid descriptions of the destruction at Hiroshima and Nagasaki had been appearing in the popular media since August 1945, but the American public's attention to them as a whole increased only after the prospect that the bomb could be used against them as well became a reality. Less than a year after the first Soviet atomic bomb test, the U.S. government had begun an effort to reassure its citizens that nuclear war was not only unlikely but also survivable. Cold War scholar Derek Leebaert recounts one of the most visible of these early efforts:

> Congress created the Federal Civil Defense Administration [FCDA] to establish community bomb shelters and to instruct people how to protect themselves in case of nuclear war. Dozens of how-to films were made and distributed. Their titles alone tell the story: *Pattern for Survival* (1950), *You Can Beat the A-Bomb* (1950), *Survival Under Atomic Attack* (1951), and the famous *Duck and Cover* (1951) with its cheery soundtrack.[4]

While the initial efforts involved reasonably simple precautionary efforts (for example, children were instructed to take cover under their desks in case a nuclear attack occurred during school hours), as the Soviet nuclear arsenal expanded, the guidelines for surviving a nuclear war became more complex (and, as many observers were quick to point out, more unrealistic).

A fallout-shelter-building craze swept the United States in the late 1950s and early 1960s, largely in response to FCDA-issued pamphlets and films that argued that such structures could allow the nation to survive a war, even in the face of massive destruction. This rationale is stated matter-of-factly in a chapter titled "How to Survive Attack and Live for Your Country's Recovery" in a civil defense booklet from late 1961:

> There is no panacea for protection from nuclear attack. In a major attack upon our country, millions of people would be killed. There appears to be no practical pro-

People protest the use of tax dollars for the development of nuclear weapons in March 1950.

gram that would avoid large-scale loss of life. But an effective program of civil defense could save the lives of millions who would not otherwise survive. Fallout shelters and related preparations, for example, could greatly reduce the number of casualties.[5]

Though these very visible preparations provided a measure of calm in the face of nuclear stockpiles that numbered into the thousands by 1960, critics were quick to claim that the actual protection provided by such shelters was questionable. Furthermore, they argued that psychological studies of survivors of the blasts at Hiroshima and Nagasaki suggested that the desire to continue living after a nuclear war might be minimal. Within two years of the height of the shelter-construction frenzy, the two rival superpowers came as close as they ever would to putting civil defense to a practical test.

The Cuban Missile Crisis

In October 1962, tensions between the United States and the Soviet Union had already been running high for more than a year over the issue of a wall built by the Soviets to separate Communist East Berlin from non-Communist West Berlin. Thus, when evidence surfaced that the Soviets were building a base designed to house nuclear missiles in Cuba, less than ninety miles from the southern tip of Florida, it touched off a thirteen-day showdown that provided the most tense moments of the Cold War. President John F. Kennedy blockaded Cuba and threatened to fire on Soviet ships that were suspected of carrying the missiles to Cuba. Soviet premier Nikita Khrushchev in turn replied that the blockade was unwarranted and was a provocation that could lead to war. Historian Spencer Weart summarizes the mood during this time:

> Among leaders and the public together, nuclear fear reached a higher peak during this crisis than at any time before or since. As Soviet ships approached the American blockade fleet, a considerable number of people from London to Tokyo thought they might not live to see another dawn. Young people in particular became deeply alarmed. The public was calm only in Moscow, where the press called for peace and did not mention until after the crisis was over that the squabble had something to do with nuclear missiles. In Washington, shovels and sandbags were sold out at hardware stores, while Pentagon employees snatched up civil defense leaflets. In some cities food hoarding panics stripped supermarkets bare.[6]

The conflict eventually subsided after Khrushchev announced that the Soviets would forgo placing the missiles in Cuba, but the experience of extreme nuclear anxiety had left both leaders sobered about the dangers of testing each other's limits in this way. Kennedy's special assistant for national security McGeorge Bundy wrote several years later about the main lesson taught by the crisis:

> The risk of nuclear war during the thirteen days was real, and the most important single consequence of the missile crisis may be that neither side wants to run such risk again. I have argued that the risk was small, given the prudence and unchallenged final control of the two leaders. . . . It might be very small indeed, but in this apocalyptic matter the risk can be very small indeed and still much too large for comfort.[7]

Both sides took steps in the years immediately following the crisis to lessen the risk of war, from largely symbolic actions such as the installation of a "hot line" telephone between the two leaders' offices to more substantive developments like the 1963 Limited Test-Ban Treaty (an agreement to stop above-ground tests of nuclear weapons).

Nuclear Anxiety Subsides . . . Temporarily

With both sides making gestures that appeared to step back from the brink of nuclear war, the anxiety surrounding the bomb also diminished in the mid- to late 1960s. Boyer notes that there was

> a sharp decline in culturally expressed engagement with the issue [of nuclear war]. . . . One might call this the Era of the Big Sleep. Public-opinion data reflect this shift. In 1959, 64 percent of Americans listed nuclear war as the nation's most urgent problem. By 1964, the figure had dropped to 16 percent. Soon it vanished entirely from the surveys. An early 1970s study of the treatment of the nuclear arms race in American educational journals found the subject almost totally ignored.[8]

Weart also notes this silence, calling it "the only documented case in history when most of the world's citizens stopped paying attention to facts that continued to threaten their very survival."[9] One major factor he mentions is the relative calm brought about by the period of détente (a French term signifying mutual agreement) that existed between the superpowers during the second half of the 1960s and most of the 1970s. Between 1965 and 1979, the United States and the Soviet Union were almost constantly engaged in highly publicized arms talks intended to reduce the size of their respective arsenals (even though both sides were still adding thousands of new warheads to their stockpiles during this time).

Also important were the pressing issues of civil rights and the Vietnam War, both of which demanded a large share of Americans' attention in the late 1960s and early 1970s, thereby distracting them from consideration of the more distant-seeming nuclear threat. Even the fact that several additional countries—France in 1960, China in 1964, India in 1974—had joined the nuclear family did not seem to cause much of a resurgence in public expressions of nuclear anxiety during the years of détente. Only when open hostility returned to U.S.-Soviet relations in the wake of the Soviets' 1979 invasion of Afghanistan did the fear of nuclear war resurface. President Jimmy Carter's decision to pull the U.S. team out of the 1980 Moscow Summer Olympics to protest the Soviet invasion symbolized the renewed atmosphere of dislike and distrust between the superpowers.

The renewed fear of Soviet aggression among the voters helped Ronald Reagan, a strident anti-Communist and a strong supporter of increased spending on nuclear weapons, defeat Carter soundly in the presidential elections of 1980. Upon taking office, Reagan adopted a hard-line position toward the Soviets, referring to them in speeches as "the Evil Empire" and spending vast amounts of money on expanding and improving the country's nuclear arsenal. His 1983 proposal to develop a space-based defense system to protect against incoming missiles threatened to undermine one of the most important treaties of the détente era, the 1972 Anti-Ballistic

Missile Treaty, which outlawed the development of defense systems designed to shoot down incoming missiles. The chief argument against such a system had been that it would destabilize the peace that existed between the superpowers since it would give one side the potential to launch a "first strike" attack against the other on the assumption that the missile defense system would reduce the amount of damage that any retaliation would cause to an acceptable level.

Although the harsh words and belligerent actions of both Reagan and his numerous Soviet counterparts in the early to mid-1980s did cause an upsurge in anxiety regarding the threat of nuclear war (as can be seen by the sharp increase in the number of articles, books, movies, and other media that deal with the subject), it also caused a dramatic increase in worldwide antinuclear activism and peace movements. There had been groups active in such protests during the 1950s and early 1960s, but the scale of such movements was much greater in the 1980s and resulted in numerous dramatic public displays of protest against nuclear weapons. Groups such as SANE/ Freeze and the Physicians for Social Responsibility helped give many people an outlet for their renewed nuclear anxiety.

Was the End of the Cold War the End of the Nuclear Threat?

The final five years of the Cold War were notable for a series of arms control agreements that, for the first time since the development of nuclear weapons, began reducing the number of warheads. After Mikhail Gorbachev took over as Soviet premier in 1985, he began an ambitious program of social and political reform within the country, moving it away from hardline communism and toward a more open society. These actions helped change the perception of the Soviet Union for many Americans—including Reagan—and greatly reduced the tensions between the superpowers, a factor that helped create an atmosphere in which nuclear arms reduction was possible.

As the Soviet Union became less of a threat in the late 1980s, the main nuclear fear for the United States became the issue of what would happen to the sizable Soviet nuclear arsenal in the case of a power struggle or the complete disintegration of the country. For many, the fear that individual nuclear weapons would fall into the hands of terrorist organizations, so-called rogue states, or other radical groups replaced the fear of all-out nuclear apocalypse. When the Soviet Union ceased to exist in 1991, its nuclear weapons were initially to be dispersed among four of the separate countries—Russia, Belarus, Ukraine, and Kazakhstan—that arose in its wake. The United States convinced these nations—largely by offering substantial sums of monetary assistance—to give up these weapons to Russia alone, since it could account for and control the weapons most effectively. Limiting the number of nuclear-armed nations (a concept known as nonproliferation) in the post–Cold War world was seen as one means of containing the new nuclear fear as much as possible. As a result, repeated threats of nuclear conflict between India and Pakistan—both of which have already developed nuclear weapons—and concerns about possible nuclear weapons in Israel, Iran, Iraq, and North Korea have been major factors in global politics in the decade-plus since the end of the Cold War.

Thus, it would be an overstatement to say that Auden's "Age of Anxiety" ended along with the Cold War. To be sure, the risk of complete nuclear annihilation has been greatly decreased, both because of nearly eightfold reductions in global nuclear stockpiles and because of the end of the hostile relations between the two nations with the largest arsenals. Nevertheless, nuclear weapons have proven to be a genie that cannot easily be put back in the bottle from which they came. As the technology required to create nuclear weapons has become more widely available, the threat that such weapons might be used has changed in nature and diminished in scale, but by no means has it disappeared.

Notes

1. Margot A. Henriksen, *Dr. Strangelove's America: Society and Culture in the Atomic Age.* Berkeley: University of California Press, 1997, p. 342.
2. Paul Boyer, *By the Bomb's Early Light: American Thought and Culture at the Dawn of the Atomic Age.* New York: Pantheon, 1985, p. 336.

3. Stephen Hilgartner, Richard C. Bell, and Rory O'Connor, *Nukespeak: Nuclear Language, Visions, and Mindset*. San Francisco: Sierra Club Books, 1982, p. 92.

4. Derek Leebaert, *The Fifty-Year Wound: The True Price of America's Cold War Victory*. Boston: Little, Brown, 2002, p. 97.

5. *Fallout Protection: What to Know and Do About Nuclear Attack*. Washington, DC: Office of Civil Defense, 1961, pp. 5–6.

6. Spencer R. Weart, *Nuclear Fear: A History of Images*. Cambridge, MA: Harvard University Press, 1988, pp. 258–59.

7. McGeorge Bundy, *Danger and Survival: Choices About the Bomb in the First Fifty Years*. New York: Vintage, 1990, p. 461.

8. Boyer, *By the Bomb's Early Light*, p. 355.

9. Weart, *Nuclear Fear*, p. 262.

CHAPTER 1

The Leaders Speak on Nuclear Weapons

Revealing the Nuclear Secret

Harry S. Truman

Prior to August 6, 1945, the secret of the atomic bomb's existence was known only to the scientists working on the classified Manhattan Project at Los Alamos, New Mexico. Once an atomic bomb had been dropped on the Japanese city of Hiroshima, though, President Harry S. Truman moved quickly to announce this fact to the American people. The public responded with a mixture of hope that the bomb would hasten the end of the war and revulsion at the unprecedented destructive power that had been unleashed. The primary purpose of his message was to threaten Japan with further atomic attacks if it did not surrender immediately and unconditionally; this threat was fulfilled three days later when Nagasaki was bombed. Many historians have argued that Truman's statement was also indirectly intended to warn the Soviet Union against taking advantage of Japan's imminent defeat to acquire new territories in Asia. Even as he issues these explicit and implicit threats, Truman does not rule out eventually making the secret of the atomic bomb available to allies. This attitude, however, quickly faded once the war ended, in part because of Truman's deep distrust of Soviet leader Joseph Stalin. In turn, the Soviet Union dramatically sped up its own bomb development program—assisted greatly by the work of spies within the Manhattan Project—and the nuclear arms race was underway.

Harry S. Truman, address to the nation, Washington, DC, August 6, 1945.

Sixteen hours ago [on August 6, 1945] an American airplane dropped one bomb on Hiroshima, an important Japanese Army base. That bomb had more power than 20,000 tons of TNT. It had more than 2,000 times the blast power of the British "Grand Slam," which is the largest bomb ever yet used in the history of warfare.

The Japanese began the war from the air at Pearl Harbor. They have been repaid manyfold. And the end is not yet. With this bomb we have now added a new and revolutionary increase in destruction to supplement the growing power of our armed forces. In their present form these bombs are now in production, and even more powerful forms are in development.

It is an atomic bomb. It is a harnessing of the basic power of the universe. The force from which the sun draws its power has been loosed against those who brought war to the Far East.

Truman Reveals the Manhattan Project

Before 1939, it was the accepted belief of scientists that it was theoretically possible to release atomic energy. But no one knew any practical method of doing it. By 1942, however, we knew that the Germans were working feverishly to find a way to add atomic energy to the other engines of war with which they hoped to enslave the world. But they failed. We may be grateful to Providence that the Germans got the V-1's and V-2's [early rockets capable of reaching Great Britain] late and in limited quantities and even more grateful that they did not get the atomic bomb at all.

The battle of the laboratories held fateful risks for us as well as the battles of the air, land, and sea, and we have now won the battle of the laboratories as we have won the other battles.

Beginning in 1940, before Pearl Harbor, scientific knowledge useful in war was pooled between the United States and Great Britain, and many priceless helps to our victories have come from that arrangement. Under that general policy the research on the atomic bomb was begun. With American and British scientists working together we entered the race of discovery against the Germans.

On August 6, 1945, the United States dropped an atomic bomb on Hiroshima, reducing the city to rubble and instantly killing some seventy thousand people.

The United States had available the large number of scientists of distinction in the many needed areas of knowledge. It had the tremendous industrial and financial resources necessary for the project, and they could be devoted to it without undue impairment of other vital war work. In the United States the laboratory work and the production plants, on which a substantial start had already been made, would be out of reach of enemy bombing, while at that time Britain was exposed to constant air attack and was still threatened with the possibility of invasion. For these reasons Prime Minister [Winston] Churchill and President [Franklin] Roosevelt agreed that it was wise to carry on the project here.

We now have two great plants and many lesser works devoted to the production of atomic power. Employment during peak construction numbered 125,000 and over 65,000 individuals are even now engaged in operating the plants. Many have worked there for two and a half years. Few know what they have been producing. They see great quantities of material going in and they see nothing coming out of these plants, for the physical size of the explosive charge is exceedingly small. We have spent $2 billion on the greatest scientific gamble in history—and won.

But the greatest marvel is not the size of the enterprise, its secrecy, nor its cost, but the achievement of scientific brains in putting together infinitely complex pieces of knowledge held by many men in different fields of science into a workable plan. And hardly less marvelous has been the capacity of industry to design, and of labor to operate, the machines and methods to do things never done before so that the brainchild of many minds came forth in physical shape and performed as it was supposed to do. Both science and industry worked under the direction of the United States Army, which achieved a unique success in managing so diverse a problem in the advancement of knowledge in an amazingly short time. It is doubtful if such another combination could be got together in the world. What has been done is the greatest achievement of organized science in history. It was done under high pressure and without failure.

Truman Uses the Atomic Bomb as a Threat

We are now prepared to obliterate more rapidly and completely every productive enterprise the Japanese have above ground in any city. We shall destroy their docks, their factories, and their communications. Let there be no mistake; we shall completely destroy Japan's power to make war.

It was to spare the Japanese people from utter destruction that the ultimatum of July 26 [1945] was issued at Potsdam [a city in eastern Germany in which Truman, Churchill, and Stalin met]. Their leaders promptly rejected that ultimatum. If they do not now accept our terms they may expect a rain of ruin from the air, the like of which has never been seen on this earth. Behind this air attack will follow sea and land forces in such numbers and power as they have not yet seen and with the fighting skill of which they are already well aware.

The secretary of war [Henry Stimson], who has kept in personal touch with all phases of the project, will immediately make public a statement giving further details.

His statement will give facts concerning the sites at Oak Ridge near Knoxville, Tennessee, and at Richland near Pasco, Washington, and an installation near Santa Fe, New Mexico. Although the workers at the sites have been making materials to be used in producing the greatest destructive force in history, they have not themselves been in danger beyond that of many other occupations, for the utmost care has been taken of their safety.

Truman's Plan for the Immediate Future

The fact that we can release atomic energy ushers in a new era in man's understanding of nature's forces. Atomic energy may in the future supplement the power that now comes from coal, oil, and falling water, but at present it cannot be produced on a basis to compete with them commercially. Before that comes there must be a long period of intensive research.

It has never been the habit of the scientists of this country or the policy of this government to withhold from the world scientific knowledge. Normally, therefore, everything about the work with atomic energy would be made public.

But under present circumstances it is not intended to divulge the technical processes of production or all the military applications, pending further examination of possible methods of protecting us and the rest of the world from the danger of sudden destruction.

I shall recommend that the Congress of the United States consider promptly the establishment of an appropriate commission to control the production and use of atomic power within the United States. I shall give further consideration and make further recommendations to the Congress as to how atomic power can become a powerful and forceful influence towards the maintenance of world peace.

Living Under the Nuclear Sword of Damocles

John F. Kennedy

In the 1960 presidential election, John F. Kennedy had campaigned as a fervent anti-Communist. His speeches in his campaign against Richard Nixon contained strong condemnations of communism and used the general fear of nuclear war to motivate the public to vote for him. For example, he claimed that a "missile gap" existed between the Soviet Union and the United States, although this was later proven untrue. After he took office, Kennedy began to strike a somewhat more conciliatory tone, which Soviet premier Nikita Khrushchev interpreted as a sign of weakness in Kennedy. During the first year of Kennedy's presidency, Khrushchev pursued policies in Berlin and Cuba that were deliberately provocative even as the two leaders publicly discussed diminishing the nuclear threat.

When Kennedy addressed the United Nations on September 25, 1961, he was being pushed both by his wish to reduce the potential for nuclear war but also by his desire to confront Khrushchev's incitements (the infamous Berlin Wall had been built a month prior to Kennedy's speech) with a firm hand. He used the metaphor of the Sword of Damocles to drive home the point of how dangerous the kind of policies being pursued by the Soviet Union in Berlin were. In Greek mythology, Damocles was a brash courtier who was taught a lesson about the fleeting nature of power

John F. Kennedy, address before the General Assembly of the United Nations, New York, September 25, 1961.

by the king of Syracuse. At a banquet, the king seated Damocles on a throne above which hung a sword that was held in place only by a single strand of hair. Kennedy used this metaphor to emphasize the false comfort that nuclear weapons gave to their possessors. Kennedy used this speech not just to chastise the Soviets for their actions in Berlin but to present a series of proposals for disarmament. It was only after the extreme nuclear tension of the Cuban Missile Crisis in October 1962 that the two sides began seriously discussing his proposals.

Today [September 25, 1961], every inhabitant of this planet must contemplate the day when this planet may no longer be habitable. Every man, woman and child lives under a nuclear sword of Damocles, hanging by the slenderest of threads, capable of being cut at any moment by accident or miscalculation or by madness. The weapons of war must be abolished before they abolish us.

Men no longer debate whether armaments are a symptom or a cause of tension. The mere existence of modern weapons— ten million times more powerful than any that the world has ever seen, and only minutes away from any target on earth—is a source of horror, and discord and distrust. Men no longer maintain that disarmament must await the settlement of all disputes —for disarmament must be a part of any permanent settlement. And men may no longer pretend that the quest for disarmament is a sign of weakness—for in a spiraling arms race, a nation's security may well be shrinking even as its arms increase.

For fifteen years this organization [the United Nations] has sought the reduction and destruction of arms. Now that goal is no longer a dream—it is a practical matter of life or death. The risks inherent in disarmament pale in comparison to the risks inherent in an unlimited arms race.

It is in this spirit that the recent Belgrade Conference [a disarmament meeting held in Yugoslavia in 1961]—recognizing that this is no longer a Soviet problem or an American problem, but a human problem—endorsed a program of "general, complete and strictly an internationally controlled disarmament."

It is in this same spirit that we in the United States have labored this year, with a new urgency, and with a new, now statutory agency fully endorsed by the Congress, to find an approach to disarmament which would be so far-reaching, yet realistic, so mutually balanced and beneficial, that it could be accepted by every nation. And it is in this spirit that we have presented with the agreement of the Soviet Union—under the label both nations now accept of "general and complete disarmament"—a new statement of newly-agreed principles for negotiation [the McCloy-Zorin Agreement].

But we are well aware that all issues of principle are not settled, and that principles alone are not enough. It is therefore our intention to challenge the Soviet Union, not to an arms race, but to a peace race—to advance together step by step, stage by stage, until general and complete disarmament has been achieved. We invite them now to go beyond agreement in principle to reach agreement on actual plans.

Another Proposal for International Arms Control

The program to be presented to this assembly—for general and complete disarmament under effective international control—moves to bridge the gap between those who insist on a gradual approach and those who talk only of the final and total achievement. It would create machinery to keep the peace as it destroys the machinery of war. It would proceed through balanced and safeguarded stages designed to give no state a military advantage over another. It would place the final responsibility for verification and control where it belongs, not with the big powers alone, not with one's adversary or one's self, but in an international organization within the framework of the United Nations. It would assure that indispensable condition of disarmament—true inspection—and apply it in stages proportionate to the stage of disarmament. It would cover delivery systems as well as weapons. It would ultimately halt their production as well as their testing, their transfer as well as their possession. It would achieve under the eyes of an international disarmament organization, a steady reduction in force, both nuclear and conventional, until it has abolished all armies and all weapons except those needed for internal order and a new United Nations Peace Force. And it starts that process now, today, even as the talks begin.

In short, general and complete disarmament must no longer be a slogan, used to resist the first steps. It is no longer to be a goal without means of achieving it, without means of verifying its progress, without means of keeping the peace. It is now a realistic plan, and a test—a test of those only willing to talk and a test of those willing to act.

Such a plan would not bring a world free from conflict and greed—but it would bring a world free from the terrors of mass destruction. It would not usher in the era of the super state—but it would usher in an era in which no state could annihilate or be annihilated by another.

In 1945, this Nation [the United States] proposed the Baruch Plan [named after diplomat Bernard Baruch, who presented it to the UN] to internationalize the atom before other nations even possessed the bomb or demilitarized their troops. We proposed with our allies the Disarmament plan of 1951 while still at war in Korea. And we make our proposals today, while building up our defenses over Berlin [a military confrontation was looming in this German city over Soviet policies in its zone of control], not because we are inconsistent or insincere or intimidated, but because we know the rights of free men will prevail—because while we are compelled against our will to rearm, we look confidently beyond Berlin to the kind of disarmed world we all prefer.

I therefore propose on the basis of this Plan, that disarmament negotiations resume promptly, and continue without interruption until an entire program for general and complete disarmament has not only been agreed but has actually been achieved.

Working Toward a Test Ban Treaty

The logical place to begin is a treaty assuring the end of nuclear tests of all kinds, in every environment, under workable controls. The United States and the United Kingdom have proposed such a treaty that is both reasonable, effective and ready for signature. We are still prepared to sign that treaty today.

We also proposed a mutual ban on atmospheric testing, without inspection or controls, in order to save the human race from the poison of radioactive fallout. We regret that the offer has not been accepted.

For 15 years we have sought to make the atom an instrument of peaceful growth rather than of war. But for 15 years our concessions have been matched by obstruction, our patience by intransigence. And the pleas of mankind for peace have met with disregard.

Finally, as the explosions of others beclouded the skies, my country was left with no alternative but to act in the interests of its own and the free world's security. We cannot endanger that security by refraining from testing while others improve their arsenals. Nor can we endanger it by another long, uninspected ban on testing. For three years [1958–1961] we accepted those risks in our open society while seeking agreement on inspection. But this year, while we were negotiating in good faith [at arms talks] in Geneva, others [i.e., the Soviet Union] were secretly preparing new experiments in destruction.

Our tests are not polluting the atmosphere. Our deterrent weapons are guarded against accidental explosion or use. Our doctors and scientists stand ready to help any nation measure and meet the hazards to health which inevitably result from the tests in the atmosphere.

Kennedy's Disarmament Proposal

But to halt the spread of these terrible weapons, to halt the contamination of the air, to halt the spiralling nuclear arms race, we remain ready to seek new avenues of agreement, our new Disarmament Program thus includes the following proposals:

—First, signing the test-ban treaty by all nations. This can be done now. Test ban negotiations need not and should not await general disarmament.

—Second, stopping the production of fissionable materials [i.e., materials that can produce atomic energy] for use in weapons, and preventing their transfer to any nation now lacking in nuclear weapons.

—Third, prohibiting the transfer of control over nuclear weapons to states that do not own them.

—Fourth, keeping nuclear weapons from seeding new battlegrounds in outer space.

—Fifth, gradually destroying existing nuclear weapons and converting their materials to peaceful uses; and

—Finally, halting the unlimited testing and production of strategic nuclear delivery vehicles, and gradually destroying them as well. . . .

A Warning and a Vision of Peace

The events and decisions of the next ten months may well decide the fate of man for the next ten thousand years. There will be no avoiding those events. There will be no appeal from these decisions. And we in this hall shall be remembered either as part of the generation that turned this planet into a flaming funeral pyre or the generation that met its vow "to save succeeding generations from the scourge of war." [Quoted from the UN Charter.]

In the endeavor to meet that vow, I pledge you every effort this Nation possesses. I pledge you that we will neither commit nor provoke aggression, that we shall neither flee nor invoke the threat of force that we shall never negotiate out of fear, we shall never fear to negotiate.

Terror is not a new weapon. Throughout history it has been used by those who could not prevail, either by persuasion or example. But inevitably they fail, either because men are not afraid to die for a life worth living, or because the terrorists themselves came to realize that free men cannot be frightened by threats, and that aggression would meet its own response. And it is in the light of that history that every nation today should know, be he friend or foe, that the United States has both the will and the weapons to join free men in standing up to their responsibilities.

But I come here today to look across this world of threats to a world of peace. In that search we cannot expect any final triumph—for new problems will always arise. We cannot expect that all nations will adopt like systems—for conformity is the jailor of freedom, and the enemy of growth. Nor can we expect to reach our goal by contrivance, by fiat [i.e., decree] or even by the wishes of all.

But however close we sometimes seem to that dark and final abyss, let no man of peace and freedom despair. For he does not stand alone. If we all can persevere, if we can in every land and office look beyond our own shores and ambitions, then surely the age will dawn in which the strong are just and the weak secure and the peace preserved.

Ladies and gentlemen of this Assembly, the decision is ours. Never have the nations of the world had so much to lose, or so much to gain. Together we shall save our planet, or together we shall perish in its flames. Save it we can—and save it we must—and then shall we earn the eternal thanks of mankind and, as peacemakers, the eternal blessing of God.

SDI: A New Strategy for Survival

Ronald Reagan

Although both the United States and Soviet Union had continued building nuclear weapons—by the early 1980s each side had over twenty thousand nuclear warheads, all of which were larger than the Hiroshima bomb —a lengthy period of relatively good relations existed between the two nations from the late 1960s until late 1979, when the Soviets invaded Afghanistan. Relations quickly deteriorated, especially after President Jimmy Carter pulled the U.S. team out of the 1980 Summer Olympics, which were being held in Moscow. Later that year, Ronald Reagan was elected president, in large part due to his hard-line stance toward the Soviet Union (which he called "the Evil Empire" in a speech). The first two years of Reagan's presidency were marked by large defense budgets aimed at modernizing and expanding the U.S. nuclear arsenal, but by 1983 Reagan had decided on a different, potentially less costly strategy, along with a greater emphasis on arms control negotiation. In a televised speech to the nation on March 23, 1983, he introduced the concept of what would come to be known as the Strategic Defense Initiative (SDI). This project was a system of antimissile defenses—including satellite-based lasers and interceptor missiles—whose intent was to protect the United States from Soviet long-range missile attacks. Reagan believed that this system would give the United States a strategic advantage. Previously, the arms race had been based on the concept of mutually assured destruction—the idea that if either side attacked,

Ronald Reagan, address to the nation, Washington, DC, March 23, 1983.

the other side would respond with full force, guaranteeing that both sides would be destroyed. With SDI, Reagan figured, the United States would remove the Soviets' first-strike capacity, allowing the Americans to both defend themselves and prevail over their enemy.

Opponents of Reagan's plan claimed that his so-called Star Wars program was not only impossible to achieve but also threatened to accelerate the arms race and to destabilize the "balance of terror" that had been achieved over the years of the Cold War through the policy of mutual nuclear deterrence. In fact, the Anti-Ballistic Missile (ABM) Treaty that had been signed in 1972 outlawed similar land-based systems, but Reagan claimed this treaty did not pertain to defenses in space. Although the system was never actually implemented, billions of dollars were spent on research and development. Some policy experts credit the threat of SDI with forcing the Soviets to negotiate on nuclear arms.

The defense policy of the United States is based on a simple premise: The United States does not start fights. We will never be an aggressor. We maintain our strength in order to deter and defend against aggression—to preserve freedom and peace.

Since the dawn of the atomic age, we've sought to reduce the risk of war by maintaining a strong deterrent and by seeking genuine arms control. "Deterrence" means simply this: making sure any adversary who thinks about attacking the United States, or our allies, or our vital interests, concludes that the risks to him outweigh any potential gains. Once he understands that, he won't attack. We maintain the peace through our strength; weakness only invites aggression.

This strategy of deterrence has not changed. It still works. But what it takes to maintain deterrence has changed. It took one kind of military force to deter an attack when we had far more nuclear weapons than any other power; it takes another kind now that the Soviets, for example, have enough accurate and powerful nuclear weapons to destroy virtually all of our missiles on the ground. Now, this is not to say that the Soviet Union is planning to make war on us. Nor do I believe a war is inevitable—quite the contrary. But what must be recognized is that our security is based on being prepared to meet all threats.

There was a time when we depended on coastal forts and artillery batteries, because, with the weaponry of that day, any attack would have had to come by sea. Well, this is a different world, and our defenses must be based on recognition and awareness of the weaponry possessed by other nations in the nuclear age.

We can't afford to believe that we will never be threatened. There have been two world wars in my lifetime. We didn't start them and, indeed, did everything we could to avoid being drawn into them. But we were ill-prepared for both. Had we been better prepared, peace might have been preserved.

For 20 years the Soviet Union has been accumulating enormous military might. They didn't stop when their forces exceeded all requirements of a legitimate defensive capability. And they haven't stopped now. During the past decade and a half [1968–1983] the Soviets have built up a massive arsenal of new strategic nuclear weapons—weapons that can strike directly at the United States.

As an example, the United States introduced its last new intercontinental ballistic missile, the Minute Man III, in 1969, and we're now dismantling our even older Titan missiles. But what has the Soviet Union done in these intervening years? Well, since 1969 the Soviet Union has built five new classes of ICBMs [intercontinental ballistic missiles], and upgraded these eight times. As a result, their missiles are much more powerful and accurate than they were several years ago, and they continue to develop more, while ours are increasingly obsolete. . . .

There was a time when we were able to offset superior Soviet numbers with higher quality, but today they are building weapons as sophisticated and modern as our own.

As the Soviets have increased their military power, they've been emboldened to extend that power. They're spreading their military influence in ways that can directly challenge our vital interests and those of our allies. . . .

Our NATO [North Atlantic Treaty Organization] allies have assumed a great defense burden, including the military draft in most countries. We're working with them and our other friends around the world to do more. Our defensive strategy means we need military forces that can move very quickly, forces that are trained and ready to respond to any emergency.

Every item in our defense program—our ships, our tanks, our planes, our funds for training and spare parts—is intended for one all-important purpose: to keep the peace. Unfortunately, a decade of neglecting our military forces had called into question our ability to do that.

When I took office in January 1981, I was appalled by what I found: American planes that couldn't fly and American ships that couldn't sail for lack of spare parts and trained personnel and insufficient fuel and ammunition for essential training. The inevitable result of all this was poor morale in our Armed Forces, difficulty in recruiting the brightest young Americans to wear the uniform, and difficulty in convincing our most experienced military personnel to stay on.

There was a real question then about how well we could meet a crisis. And it was obvious that we had to begin a major modernization program to ensure we could deter aggression and preserve the peace in the years ahead.

We had to move immediately to improve the basic readiness and staying power of our conventional forces, so they could meet—and therefore help deter—a crisis. We had to make up for lost years of investment by moving forward with a long-term plan to prepare our forces to counter the military capabilities our adversaries were developing for the future.

I know that all of you want peace, and so do I. I know too that many of you seriously believe that a nuclear freeze would further the cause of peace. But a freeze now would make us less, not more, secure and would raise, not reduce, the risks of war. It would be largely unverifiable and would seriously undercut our negotiations on arms reduction. It would reward the Soviets for their massive military buildup while preventing us from modernizing our aging and increasingly vulnerable forces. With their present margin of superiority, why should they agree to arms reductions knowing that we were prohibited from catching up?

Believe me, it wasn't pleasant for someone who had come to Washington determined to reduce government spending, but we had to move forward with the task of repairing our defenses or we would lose our ability to deter conflict now and in the future. We had to demonstrate to any adversary that aggression could not succeed, and that the only real solution was substantial, equitable, and effectively verifiable arms reduction—the kind we're working for right now [at ongoing arms control talks] in Geneva. . . .

Changing the Strategy

Now, thus far tonight I've shared with you my thoughts on the problems of national security we must face together. My predecessors in the Oval Office have appeared before you on other occasions to describe the threat posed by Soviet power and have proposed steps to address that threat. But since the advent of nuclear weapons, those steps have been increasingly directed toward deterrence of aggression through the promise of retaliation.

This approach to stability through offensive threat has worked. We and our allies have succeeded in preventing nuclear war for more than three decades. In recent months, however, my advisers, including in particular the Joint Chiefs of Staff [the top-ranking officers of each branch of the military] have underscored the necessity to break out of a future that relies solely on offensive retaliation for our security.

Over the course of these discussions, I've become more and more deeply convinced that the human spirit must be capable of rising above dealing with other nations and human beings by threatening their existence. Feeling this way, I believe we must thoroughly examine every opportunity for reducing tensions and for introducing greater stability into the strategic calculus on both sides.

One of the most important contributions we can make is, of course, to lower the level of all arms, and particularly nuclear arms. We're engaged right now in several negotiations with the Soviet Union to bring about a mutual reduction of weapons. I will report to you a week from tomorrow my thoughts on that score. But let me just say, I'm totally committed to this course.

If the Soviet Union will join with us in our effort to achieve major arms reduction, we will have succeeded in stabilizing the nuclear balance. Nevertheless, it will still be necessary to rely on the specter of retaliation, on mutual threat. And that's a sad commentary on the human condition. Wouldn't it be better to save lives than to avenge them? Are we not capable of demonstrating our peaceful intentions by applying all our abilities and our ingenuity to achieving a truly lasting stability? I think we are. Indeed, we must.

The Strategic Defense Initiative

After careful consultation with my advisers, including the Joint Chiefs of Staff, I believe there is a way. Let me share with you a vision of the future which offers hope. It is that we embark on a program to counter the awesome Soviet missile threat with measures that are defensive. Let us turn to the very strengths in technology that spawned our great industrial base and that have given us the quality of life we enjoy today.

What if free people could live secure in the knowledge that their security did not rest upon the threat of instant U.S. retaliation to deter a Soviet attack, that we could intercept and destroy strategic ballistic missiles before they reached our own soil or that of our allies?

I know this is a formidable, technical task, one that may not be accomplished before the end of this century. Yet, current technology has attained a level of sophistication where it's reasonable for us to begin this effort. It will take years, probably decades of effort on many fronts. There will be failures and setbacks, just as there will be successes and breakthroughs. And as we proceed, we must remain constant in preserving the nuclear deterrent and maintaining a solid capability for flexible response. But isn't it worth every investment necessary to free the world from the threat of nuclear war? We know it is.

In the meantime, we will continue to pursue real reductions in nuclear arms, negotiating from a position of strength that can be ensured only by modernizing our strategic forces. At the same time, we must take steps to reduce the risk of a conventional military conflict escalating to nuclear war by improving our nonnuclear capabilities.

America does possess—now—the technologies to attain very significant improvements in the effectiveness of our conventional, nonnuclear forces. Proceeding boldly with these new technologies, we can significantly reduce any incentive that the Soviet Union may have to threaten attack against the United States or its allies.

Heading Off Criticism in Advance

As we pursue our goal of defensive technologies, we recognize that our allies rely upon our strategic offensive power to deter attacks against them. Their vital interests and ours are inextricably linked. Their safety and ours are one. And no change in technology can or will alter that reality. We must and shall continue to honor our commitments.

I clearly recognize that defensive systems have limitations and raise certain problems and ambiguities. If paired with offensive systems, they can be viewed as fostering an aggressive policy, and no one wants that. But with these considerations firmly in mind, I call upon the scientific community in our country, those who gave us nuclear weapons, to turn their great talents now to the cause of mankind and world peace, to give us the means of rendering these nuclear weapons impotent and obsolete.

Tonight, consistent with our obligations of the ABM [Anti-Ballistic Missile] treaty [signed in 1972, this agreement outlawed missile-based defense systems against ICBMs] and recognizing the need for closer consultation with our allies, I'm taking an important first step. I am directing a comprehensive and intensive effort to define a long-term research and development program to begin to achieve our ultimate goal of eliminating the threat posed by strategic nuclear missiles. This could pave the way for arms control measures to eliminate the weapons themselves. We seek neither military superiority nor political advantage. Our only purpose—one all people share—is to search for ways to reduce the danger of nuclear war.

A Proposal to Eliminate Nuclear Weapons

Mikhail Gorbachev

Mikhail Gorbachev was a different kind of Soviet leader. He became general secretary of the Communist Party in March 1985 after the death of Konstantin Chernenko, the last in a series of three old-guard Communists to have been in power. Gorbachev quickly set a new tone as a leader, making clear gestures toward peace with the United States and suggesting that the Soviet Union needed to undergo drastic social and economic transformations if it was to continue. His glasnost (openness) and perestroika (restructuring) reform programs expanded freedom of the press and private business, respectively. Although Gorbachev's opponents within the Soviet Union charged that he was destroying the principles of communism with his reforms, he quickly gained a great deal of popularity, not just at home but in the United States as well. One realm in which Gorbachev was especially active was disarmament.

In this statement from January 15, 1986, he went so far as to propose a plan for the complete elimination of nuclear weapons by the year 2000. He lays out the three stages of his proposal, taking into account the need for a gradual process of building up trust after more than forty years of Cold War. Though Gorbachev's proposal was undoubtedly idealistic in assuming the cooperation of not just

Mikhail Gorbachev, statement to the General Secretary of the CPSU Central Committee, Moscow, January 15, 1986.

the two superpowers but also the ten other nations that had produced nuclear weapons by the mid-1980s, his plan represented a genuine vision for eliminating nuclear weapons. Reagan and Gorbachev discussed this proposal when they met in October 1986 in Reykjavik, Iceland, but it was eventually replaced by a series of smaller, yet still substantial, arms reduction agreements that were signed between 1987 and 1991, when the Soviet Union ceased to exist.

A new year, 1986, has begun. It will be an important year, one might say a turning point in the history of the Soviet state, the year of the 27th Congress of the CPSU [Communist Party of the Soviet Union]. The Congress will chart the guidelines for the political, social, economic and intellectual development of Soviet society in the period up to the next millennium. It will adopt a programme for accelerating our peaceful construction.

All efforts of the CPSU are directed towards ensuring a further improvement of the life of the Soviet people.

A turn for the better is also needed on the international scene. This is the expectation and the demand of the peoples of the Soviet Union and of the peoples throughout the world.

Being aware of this, at the very start of the new year the Political Bureau of the CPSU Central Committee and the Soviet Government have adopted a decision on a number of major foreign policy measures that are of a fundamental nature. They are designed to promote to a maximum degree an improvement of the international situation. They are prompted by the need to overcome the negative confrontational tendencies that have been growing in recent years and to clear the ways towards curbing the nuclear arms race on earth and preventing it in outer space, towards an overall reduction of the war danger and towards confidence-building as an integral part of relations among states.

A Proposal for Eliminating Nuclear Weapons

The most important of these measures is a concrete programme aimed at the complete elimination of nuclear weapons throughout the world within a precisely defined period of time.

The Soviet Union proposes that a step-by-step, consistent process of ridding the earth of nuclear weapons be implemented and completed within the next 15 years, before the end of this century.

The 20th century has given mankind the gift of the energy of the atom. However, the great achievement of the human intellect can turn into an instrument of mankind's self-annihilation.

Is it possible to resolve this contradiction? We are convinced that it is possible. Finding effective ways of eliminating nuclear weapons is a feasible task, provided it is tackled without delay.

The Soviet Union proposes that a programme of ridding mankind of the fear of a nuclear catastrophe be carried out beginning in 1986. The fact that this year has been proclaimed by the United Nations the International Year of Peace provides an additional political and moral stimulus for this. What is required here is that we should rise above national selfishness, tactical considerations, differences and disputes, whose significance is nothing compared to the preservation of what is most cherished—peace and a secure future. The energy of the atom should be placed solely at the service of peace, a goal that our socialist state has consistently pursued and continues to pursue.

Our country was the first to raise, back in 1946, the question of prohibiting the production and use of atomic weapons and to make nuclear energy serve peaceful purposes, for the benefit of mankind.

How does the Soviet Union envisage today in practical terms the process of reducing nuclear weapons, both delivery vehicles and warheads, up to their complete elimination? Our proposals on this subject can be summarized as follows.

The First Step Toward Disarmament

Stage One. Within the next 5 to 8 years the USSR and the USA will reduce by one half the nuclear weapons that can reach each other's territory. As for the remaining delivery vehicles of this kind, each side will retain no more than 6000 warheads.

It stands to reason that such a reduction is possible only if both the USSR and the USA renounce the development, testing and deployment of space-strike weapons. As the Soviet Union has repeatedly warned, the development of space-strike weapons will dash the hopes for a reduction of nuclear armaments on earth.

The first stage will include the adoption and implementation of a decision on the complete elimination of medium-range missiles of the USSR and the USA in the European zone—both ballistic and cruise missiles—as a first step towards ridding the European continent of nuclear weapons.

At the same time the United States should undertake not to transfer its strategic and medium-range missiles to other countries, while Britain and France should pledge not to build up their respective nuclear arsenals.

The USSR and the USA should from the very beginning agree to stop all nuclear explosions and call upon other states to join in such a moratorium as soon as possible.

The reason why the first stage of nuclear disarmament should concern the Soviet Union and the United States is that it is they who should set an example for the other nuclear powers. We said that very frankly to President Reagan of the United States during our meeting in Geneva.

The Next Step

Stage Two. At this stage, which should start no later than 1990 and last for 5 to 7 years, the other nuclear powers will begin to join the process of nuclear disarmament. To start with, they would pledge to freeze all their nuclear arms and not to have them on the territories of other countries.

In this period the USSR and the USA will continue to carry out the reductions agreed upon during the first stage and also implement further measures aimed at eliminating their medium-range nuclear weapons and freezing their tactical nuclear systems.

Following the completion by the USSR and the USA of 50-per-cent reduction of their respective armaments at the second stage, another radical step will be taken: all nuclear powers will eliminate their tactical nuclear weapons, i.e., weapons having a range (or radius of action) of up to 1000 kilometres [600 miles].

At this stage the Soviet-US accord on the prohibition of space-strike weapons would become multilateral, with the mandatory participation in it of the major industrial powers.

All nuclear powers would stop nuclear weapon tests.

There would be a ban on the development of non-nuclear weapons based on new physical principles, whose destructive power is close to that of nuclear arms or other weapons of mass destruction.

The Last Step to Complete Nuclear Disarmament

Stage Three will begin no later than 1995. At this stage the elimination of all remaining nuclear weapons will be completed. By the end of 1999 there will be no nuclear weapons on earth. A universal accord will be drawn up that such weapons should never again come into being.

We envisage that special procedures will be worked out for the destruction of nuclear weapons as well as for the dismantling, conversion or scrapping of delivery vehicles. In the process, agreement will be reached on the number of weapons to be scrapped at each stage, the sites of their destruction and so on.

Verification of the destruction or limitation of arms could be carried out both by national technical means and through on-site inspections. The USSR is ready to reach agreement on any other additional verification measures.

Adoption of the nuclear disarmament programme that we are proposing would unquestionably have a favourable impact on the negotiations conducted at bilateral and multilateral forums. The programme would envisage clearly-defined routes and reference points, establish a specific timetable for achieving agreements and implementing them and would make the negotiations purposeful and task-oriented. This would stop the dangerous trend whereby the momentum of the arms race is greater than the progress of negotiations.

Thus, we propose that we should enter the third millennium without nuclear weapons, on the basis of mutually acceptable and strictly verifiable agreements. If the United States

Administration is indeed committed to the goal of the complete elimination of nuclear weapons everywhere, as it has repeatedly stated, it now has a real opportunity to carry it out in practice. Instead of spending the next 10 to 15 years in developing new space weapons, which are extremely dangerous for mankind, weapons, allegedly designed to make nuclear arms useless, would it not be more sensible to start eliminating those weapons and finally doing away with them altogether? The Soviet Union, I repeat, proposes precisely that.

The Soviet Union calls upon all peoples and states, and, naturally, above all nuclear states, to support the programme of eliminating nuclear weapons before the year 2000. It is absolutely clear to any unbiased person that if such a programme is implemented, nobody would lose and all stand to gain. This is a problem common to all mankind and it can and must be solved only through joint efforts. And the sooner this programme is translated into practical deeds, the safer life on our planet will be. . . .

How the Proposal Would Affect Arms Control Talks

In order to implement the programme of reducing and eliminating nuclear arsenals, it is necessary to activate the entire existing system of negotiations and to ensure the highest possible efficiency of the disarmament mechanism.

In a few days the Soviet-American talks on nuclear and space arms will be resumed in Geneva. When we met with President [Ronald] Reagan last November in Geneva, we had a frank discussion on the whole range of problems which are the subject of those negotiations, namely on space, strategic offensive armaments and medium-range nuclear systems. It was agreed that the negotiations should be accelerated and this agreement must not remain a mere declaration.

The Soviet delegation in Geneva will be instructed to act in strict compliance with that agreement. We expect the same constructive approach from the US side, above all on the question of space. Space must remain peaceful, strike weapons must not be deployed there. Neither must they be developed.

And there must also be introduced very strict control, including the opening of relevant laboratories for inspection.

Preventing an Arms Race in Space

Mankind is at a crucial stage of the new space age. And it is time to abandon the thinking of the stone age, when the chief concern was to have a bigger stick or a heavier stone. We are against weapons in space. Our material and intellectual capabilities make it possible for the Soviet Union to develop any weapon if we are compelled to do so. But we are fully aware of our responsibility to the present and future generations. It is our profound conviction that we should approach the third millennium not with the Star Wars programme [i.e., the Strategic Defense Initiative], but with large-scale projects of peaceful space exploration by all mankind. We propose to start practical work in developing and implementing such projects. This is one of the most important ways of ensuring progress on our entire planet and establishing a reliable system of security for all.

To prevent the arms race from spreading to outer space means to remove the obstacle barring the way to drastic reductions in nuclear weapons. On the negotiating table in Geneva is a Soviet proposal to reduce by one half the corresponding nuclear arms of the Soviet Union and the United States, which would be an important step towards the complete elimination of nuclear weapons. To block all possibility of resolving the problem of space indicates a lack of desire to stop the arms race on earth. This should be stated in clear and straightforward terms. It is not by chance that the proponents of the nuclear arms race are also ardent supporters of the Star Wars programme. These are two sides of the same policy, hostile to the interests of people.

Let me turn to the European aspect of the nuclear problem. It is a matter of extreme concern that in defiance of reason and contrary to the national interests of the European peoples, American first-strike missiles continue to be deployed in certain West European countries. This problem has been under discussion for many years now. Meanwhile the security situation in Europe continues to deteriorate.

It is time to put an end to this course of events and cut this Gordian knot [i.e., solve this difficult issue]. The Soviet Union has long been proposing that Europe should be freed of both medium-range and tactical nuclear weapons. This proposal remains valid. As a first radical step in this direction we now propose, as I have said, that even at the first stage of our programme all medium-range ballistic and cruise missiles of the USSR and the USA in the European zone should be eliminated.

The achievement of tangible practical results at the Geneva talks would give meaningful material substance to our programme to eliminate nuclear arms completely by the year 2000. . . .

Why Disarmament Should Be a Priority

Our new proposals are addressed to the entire world. Initiating active steps to halt the arms race and reduce weapons is a necessary prerequisite for coping with increasingly acute global problems—those of the deteriorating state of man's environment and of the need to find new energy sources and combat economic backwardness, hunger and disease. The pattern imposed by militarism—arms in place of development—must be replaced by the reverse order of things—disarmament for development. The noose of the trillion-dollar foreign debt, currently strangling dozens of countries and entire continents, is a direct consequence of the arms race. The more than [250 billion dollars] annually siphoned out of the developing countries is practically equal to the size of the mammoth US military budget. Indeed, this is no chance coincidence.

The Soviet Union wants each measure limiting and reducing arms and each step towards eliminating nuclear weapons not only to bring nations greater security but also to make it possible to allocate more funds for improving people's life. It is natural that the peoples seeking to put an end to backwardness and rise to the level of industrially developed countries associate the prospects of freeing themselves from the burden of foreign debt to imperialism, which is draining their economies, with limiting and eliminating weapons, reducing military expenditures and transferring resources to the goals of social and economic development. This subject will undoubtedly figure most prominently at the international conference on disarmament and development to be held in Paris next summer. . . .

There is no shortage today of statements professing commitment to peace. What is in short supply are concrete actions to strengthen foundations of peace. All too often peaceful words conceal war preparations and power politics. Moreover, some statements made from high rostrums are in fact intended to eliminate any trace of that new "spirit of Geneva" which is having a salutary effect on international relations today. It is not only a matter of statements. There are also actions clearly designed to incite animosity and mistrust, to revive confrontation, the antithesis of detente.

We reject such a way of acting and thinking. We want 1986 to be not just a peaceful year but one that will enable us to reach the end of the 20th century under the sign of peace and nuclear disarmament. The set of new foreign policy initiatives we are proposing is intended to make it possible for mankind to approach the year 2000 under peaceful skies and with a peaceful outer space, without fear of nuclear, chemical or any other threat of annihilation and fully confident of its own survival and of the continuation of the human race.

CHAPTER 2

Cultural Aspects of the Nuclear Threat

Controlling Nuclear Fears in the Early 1950s

Lisle A. Rose

Lisle A. Rose served with the U.S. Department of State from 1972 to 1989 and has taught at Johns Hopkins University's School of Advanced International Studies. In this excerpt, he discusses the fears that the potential for nuclear war caused in children during the earliest years of the Cold War. The Soviet Union tested its first atomic bomb in 1949, thereby ending the U.S. monopoly on the weapon and making the previously hypothetical danger of nuclear war more imminent for the American public. Rose looks at some of the efforts that governments—national, state, and local—undertook in an effort to reduce the rapidly growing anxiety, from civil defense training programs to instructions not to discuss certain "unpalatable" topics related to the bomb and nuclear war in classrooms. Rose focuses especially on the degree to which atomic anxiety took root in children, in part because of the conflicting messages delivered to them by civil defense programs and by popular culture.

In 1950, the cold war finally came home to Main Street America, and the nation began to fully experience its awful pressures.

The bomb instilled a quiet panic, especially among the young, who would come to maturity in the sixties and early seventies. In a confusing spasm of compassion and concern, adult Americans tried to both warn and soothe their children about nuclear warfare. The effort failed dismally. In August of the midcentury year, school systems in such "target cities" as New York, Los Angeles, Chicago, Detroit, Milwaukee, Fort Worth, San Francisco, and Philadelphia made plans to imple- ment a civil defense system and soon conducted "cover drills," during which teachers in the middle of a classroom discussion would suddenly yell "Drop!" The drills were harrowing to the children. Years later, novelist Mary Mackey remembered those terrifying moments as she and her classmates waited for the enemy A-bombs to fall: "Obediently we would fold our bodies into that attitude of prayer and supplication known only to the children of the fifties: legs folded, head between the knees, hands raised to protect the fragile, invisible nerve that floated somewhere in the blackness behind our eyes." [Historian JoAnne Brown notes that] to ensure that their students under- stood the seriousness of the exercise, "teachers passed out maps of cities upon which were superimposed ominous bulls- eyes showing the lethal reach of the bomb." [Historian Lan- don Y. Jones wrote that] baby boomers, as they would soon be called, "never forgot the lesson that their world could some- day end in a flash of light and heat while they were crouched helplessly in gyms and basements among heating ducts and spare blackboards."

A handful of critics were appalled. A university professor [quoted by Brown] complained that the press "abounds . . . in pictures of teachers standing grimly erect over children pros- trate in cover-drill." Another observer said it was unnerving to see schoolchildren searching the skies for Soviet bombers. But such characterizations of "overwrought, anxious" teachers, students, and parents were rare, and the critics were almost re- flexively reviled as subversives or worse, so the children con- tinued to suffer horrifying rituals and dreams. [A "baby boomer" quoted by Jones stated,] "At night I would lie awake in my bed and count slowly to twenty-five as each plane passed over, afraid to miss the flash of light that would be my only warning." Another survivor of a fifties childhood later wrote

A kindergarten schoolteacher in Chicago leads her pupils during an air raid drill in 1954.

[in a passage quoted by Jones] that between the ages of ten and twenty he experienced "fairly regular nightmares about the destruction of the world with nuclear weapons. These dreams almost always began with a flash of dazzling light" and continued with a "murky series of episodes in which I stumbled through rubble" looking for friend or family "whom I could never find. Often I was chased by sinister figures, but my legs could hardly move."

Trying to Reduce Atomic Anxiety

Misplaced zeal and sensitivity induced educational leaders and journalists to cloak the horrors of nuclear warfare in calmness and rationality. The National Parent-Teachers Association (PTA), following government guidelines and advice, was determined to "domesticate" the bomb, to remove its terror and make life with it livable, calm, even carefree. Parents were urged to develop a "positive mental health program" in response to their own and their children's atomic anxieties. Education journalists refused to discuss unpalatable realities of an atomic or thermonuclear blitz such as mass death, injuries, shock, blindness, burns, radiation sickness, and total social dislocation. At the beginning of the 1951 school year, soon after [President Harry] Truman announced the establishment of a Federal Civil Defense Administration, Los Angeles, New York, and other systems across the country handed out "dog tags" [military-style identification badges] to schoolboys and identification necklaces to schoolgirls. The larger cities provided the tags and necklaces free of charge. In smaller urban areas, such as Seattle and Denver, either the PTA or the Board of Education found the money to make and distribute individual identification discs. Educators from across the country met at the Civil Defense Staff College in Maryland to consider other forms of identification in case of a nuclear or thermonuclear holocaust. Tattooing was considered but rejected because of its recent "associations" [the Nazis had used tattoos to mark prisoners during the Holocaust] and its "impermanence in the case of severe burns."

Historian JoAnne Brown concluded that for anxiety-ridden adults this mass exercise in denial apparently worked. The nation's children seemed to stop worrying and begin to accept, if not love, the bomb, and civil defense became "a way of life in the schools" and by extension in the country at large. But as the years passed, appearances proved to have been deceiving. "Anger, fear, and disillusionment" followed the school generation of the fifties into young adulthood with often devastating results for itself and the country.

While the nation's educators and politicians tried to shield their young charges from the realities of nuclear war, some business people saw the issue as a means to big money. Before midcentury, communist plots and agents had vied with various exotic criminal elements as villains in comic books, which were a staple of young life before television. After 1950, comic book demons were almost invariably Commies out to destroy the

American way of life through deceit, disloyalty, and violence. In 1951, the Bowman Gum Company of Philadelphia, which had been known for issuing an annual series of stylish baseball cards to America's youth, brought out a new set of more than seventy pasteboards titled "Children's Crusade against Communism." Several front covers depicted the leaders of communism in suitably devilish style. Others showed scenes of communist-inspired or -directed mayhem or, most chilling of all, of communist mayhem to come. Card number 21, for example, titled "Mined Harbor," pictured ships blowing up and spewing irradiated shrapnel all over frightened yard workers as they sought to escape. "We know that the Reds have the atom bomb," the text on the back of the card told the kids. "In a war with the Soviet Union we would have to watch the skies for atomic raiders. But that is not all. We would have to be equally alert at the waterfront" because a "leading scientist has warned us that tramp steamers could plant A-bombs in our harbors" and "just one atomic explosion could spread ruin through an entire port." Such things were not "sure to happen. We still hope for world peace." But the not too subtle message was that the hope was pretty forlorn. One way to retain peace was to make and keep the country not only strong but alert. The price of survival was eternal vigilance.

Civil Defense and the Media

Margot A. Henriksen

In the 1950s, before nuclear stockpiles became so large that the notion of surviving a nuclear attack became unrealistic, the U.S. government spent a great deal of time and money preparing a civil defense system that was designed specifically to help minimize the casualties and chaos in the wake of a nuclear attack. The idea of civil defense programs was a holdover from World War II, when such programs were instituted in Great Britain and the United States—especially after Germany began large-scale bombing of British cities in 1940—to protect urban populations against enemy air raids.

Margot A. Henriksen, associate professor of history at the University of Hawaii, analyzes the civil defense programs of the late 1940s and early 1950s, especially in terms of debates that took place within the popular media about the possible effectiveness, necessity, and desirability of such programs. Henriksen looks at some of the high-profile articles that were used to introduce the notion of nuclear civil defense to the American people, a process that accelerated dramatically in 1950 because of the Soviets' successful test of an atomic bomb and the outbreak of the Korean War. Henriksen's conclusion is that civil defense programs were hampered not only by conflicting views among the government officials and scientists in charge of putting them together, but also by doubts that they would even work. She notes that civil defense plans were constantly being revised with each advance in atomic technology, and plans were rarely set into motion before being rendered obsolete, thus creating further doubts that civil defense would be of much use in the event of a nuclear war.

Hiroshima and Nagasaki, the Bikini test [nuclear arms test on the Bikini atoll in Micronesia], and the government's own statements about the vast power of the atom bomb all provided early evidence for the psychological and physical danger of living with the bomb, but the most consistent forum for the presentation of Americans' vulnerability belonged to the promoters of civil defense. Whether sponsored by the government or by independent groups of scientists or schoolteachers, discussions about civil defense measures emphasized the tremendous destructive potential of a nuclear weapon for an unprotected society. Even though some Americans had expressed fears of atomic destruction and the need for civil defense before 1949, the debate over civil defense gained force and added urgency after the Soviet atomic explosion in September of that year and again after the American and Soviet hydrogen bomb tests in the years between 1952 and 1954. From 1949 each new development in atomic weaponry (for example, the perfecting of the intercontinental missile) and each discovery of new dangers (for example, the lethality of radioactive fallout) fueled the controversy about America's lack of defense against atomic attack. Civil defense programs foundered with the exponential increase in the destructiveness of atomic and hydrogen bombs and missiles, but remaining at the heart of each proposal for civil defense was the concept of shelter: the shelter of a school desk for children in "duck and cover" drills, the shelter of physical distance provided in evacuation plans, or the sanctuary of underground blast and fallout shelters. By riveting attention on the need for shelter, particularly underground shelter, civil defense produced an expressive metaphor for a society divided: normal and unconcerned inhabitants above ground and cowering denizens of chambers of fear and worry underground.

Plans for civil defense explicitly recognized the split nature of life in the atomic age and openly addressed issues usually relegated to the quietly anxious mind of America, issues that most Americans had managed to shield themselves from in their lives of affluent consumerism. The notion of needing civil defense on an everyday basis was a relatively novel idea for Americans habituated to peace and geographic security, and civil defense therefore served for many Americans as an introduction to a new, potentially violent, and insecure way of life: Americans were in grave danger from atomic attack and from their own apathy about that danger; human life was devalued and threatened at all times, for sudden attack, the possibility of death, even a complete apocalypse, was omnipresent. Survival mandated facing these dangers and preparing for retreat underground. . . .

The Atomic Jitters Set In

In the tumultuous wake of the Soviet atomic explosion and the beginning of hostilities in Korea *Newsweek* commented that "the big debate was whether America should use the A-bomb. But what happened if somebody used it on us?" According to the magazine, America's civil defenses were in a mess: "Not a city or a state was ready to take an atomic attack." A week later *Newsweek* still complained that "while the whole country jittered about lack of preparation in case of atomic attack, the civil defense program was still in the talk stage in Washington last week." Given the aroused public anxieties and the clear paucity of civil defense programs at this time, President Truman pushed to establish the Federal Civil Defense Administration (FCDA) in the waning days of 1950, although the FCDA was not actually constituted until January 12, 1951. In these early "jittery" years Americans learned all about civil defense from the FCDA, the scientists, and popular magazines—why it was necessary, what forms it would take, and how Americans needed to behave to make it work. In the process they also learned just how unprotected they were.

In its December 18, 1950, issue *Life* magazine published an in-depth article called "How U.S. Cities Can Prepare for Atomic War." The introduction to the piece captured the tense mood of the nation: "As the Russian-sponsored armies of Communist

China smashed southward through Korea last week the growing likelihood of World War III posed a threat to this nation
which its cities and civilians have never had to face before. War
with Russia would be atomic war. And U.S. cities are the most
destructible targets in the world." The article proceeded to describe the destruction and panic that would accompany an
atomic attack, a feature that became a mainstay of civil defense proposals and articles:

> The particular vulnerability of big American cities to
> atomic weapons stems from a combination of two fac-
> tors: the intense congestion of the cities and the immense
> destructive power of the bomb. . . . First would come
> the immediate and total devastation of a large area, with
> casualties running into the hundreds of thousands. This
> would be the initial blow, terrible enough in itself, yet
> possibly less terrible than what would follow. Trans-
> portation would be paralyzed, power and water cut off,
> food supplies destroyed. The people would abandon the
> city in disorganized, panic-ridden flight. . . . In all, the
> indirect effects of the burst could well be more disas-
> trous than its initial destruction, for the great city would
> act as a great explosive, triggered by the lesser explosion
> of the bomb itself.

Critical of the government's inadequate planning for civil defense, *Life* devoted this article to a plan created by MIT professor Norbert Wiener which would solve the problem of urban
vulnerability to atomic attack and postbomb panic. Like [noted
chemist Eugene] Rabinowitch's proposal [Rabinowitch had
made a similar proposal in 1950], Wiener's plan focused on the
need to decentralize urban areas and to create "life belts" and
"safety zones" around cities in order to facilitate escape and
provide a destination and shelter for evacuees. The plan had
the advantage of encouraging the trend to suburbanization; indeed, the "safety zones" that bordered the escape highways
bore an uncanny resemblance to suburbia: "Nearby land will
be reserved as parks and made ready for large tent cities which
could quickly be erected to shelter the refugees. Supermarkets,

suburban homes, and small businesses would be permitted to grow up near the life belt to supplement the emergency rations and housing set up for a fleeing population."

Life made the specific connection between civil defense and suburbia, and the magazine saw the useful wartime and peacetime applications of Wiener's plan. Not only would it provide strengthened defense against atomic attack but "in peace it would expand and accelerate the current trend of many city dwellers toward the suburbs and help relieve the traffic congestion which plagues most U.S. cities." Civil defense plans like these suggested a particular atomic age rationale for the American retreat to the suburbs, and such plans helped to taint the otherwise innocent and safe quality of life in the suburbs. While the suburbs were seen as somewhat protected from the initial terrors of an atomic blast (at least until the H-bomb and its radioactive fallout revised this vision of suburb safety), they nonetheless reflected the insecurity of the age in their potential roles as sanctuaries for the bombed out and psychologically dislocated survivors of urban atomic war.

Civil Defense and Atomic Anxiety

Civil defense proposals revealed an awareness of the vast psychological problems that would accompany an atomic attack, and one Los Angeles psychiatrist offered some ideas about mental civil defense. The *Science News Letter* on January 27, 1951, highlighted Dr. Kurt Fantl's plans for what he termed "mental first aid," which included preparing "trailer first-aid stations for emergency treatment of mental casualties." Dr. Fantl suggested that these first-aid trailers "be equipped to provide restraint for acute cases as well as quick sedation to quiet over-strained nerves." Besides these measures, the psychiatrist urged preatomic war precautions against panic through the provision of shelters and through education of the public—albeit a necessarily calming sort of education:

> Panic may be prevented before disaster strikes by providing adequate shelters and lighting them with flashlights, and by education. The education should be provided

carefully so that it will not create the panic it is intended to prevent. Informing the public of dangers without a master plan to help each individual to find an actual place in the defense may actually create panic.

. . . On March 30, 1953, *Newsweek* reported on an atomic test used by the FCDA "to thus remind the American public of what even a small A-bomb could do to a typical U.S. community," but the magazine also quoted a study that estimated the cost of achieving effective civil defense measures against such A-bombs at $42 billion or $43 billion. In the cost-conscious Republican administration of [President Dwight] Eisenhower, such spending seemed highly unlikely, but *Newsweek* stated the no-win character of the situation: "The study posed a double-edged question to the Administration: Can the U.S. afford to make such an outlay; and can it afford not to?" The government opted not to approve the funds for a thorough civil defense program, and popular periodicals continued to bemoan the lack of government consistency and spending. The *Bulletin of Atomic Scientists* documented the actual decline in civil defense spending between 1952 ($153.6 million) and 1953 ($79.6 million), and the *New Republic* complained that "our civil defense program is lagging." The divisions in attitude on civil defense, on its cost and its necessity, intensified and expanded as America fully entered the hydrogen age after the March 1954 hydrogen bomb tests at the Bikini atoll in the Pacific.

In its coverage of the H-bomb blasts at Bikini—blasts frighteningly more powerful than expected—*Newsweek* included a cartoon that summed up the impact of the hydrogen bomb. The world is pictured with one arm covering its eyes and the other shaking hands with a representative of mankind, who carries with him "the ultimate super bomb." As the nearby planets plug their ears, the world says to mankind: "It was nice knowing you." The H-bomb's potential for annihilation prompted yet another contrary division in civil defense attitudes. On one hand, the hydrogen bomb made civil defense seem even more urgent and necessary, and on the other, it made any defense seem inadequate and any chance of survival negligible. *Newsweek* called attention to the latter viewpoint. Its special section on the H-bomb opened with a somber statement: "If you live in a strategically important city, the odds against your survival in an H-bomb war would be about a million to one. If you live in the country, your chances obviously would be better. But wherever you live, much of what you live for would be destroyed." After sifting through the horrible information on the H-bomb and assessing the slow progress made in civil defense to date, *Newsweek* concluded its report by stating the dire reality of the hydrogen age: "All the reports and all the statistics added up to one grim conclusion: In an atomic attack, the front would be everywhere. Every home, every factory, every school might be the target. Nobody would be secure in the H-bomb age."

The *Newsweek* story also gave some space to official government recognition of the necessity for an intensified and reformulated domestic defense program in light of the H-bomb. The magazine noted: "Taking stock of the nation's defense situation, officials conceded last week that American cities were vulnerable to attack by enemy bombers and that, if successfully attacked with the latest type of H-bombs, their populations would be virtually exterminated." The head of the FCDA, Val Peterson, vowed to pursue the new civil defense policy of "mass evacuation" with alacrity, because few options were left: "We think that if a hydrogen bomb is exploded over your city, there is only one way you can be certain of saving your life, and that is not to be in the city.". . .

H-Bomb Fallout Changes Civil Defense Thinking

When the dangers of radioactive fallout became public knowledge in the months after the H-bomb test in Bikini . . . even Rabinowitch's dispersal plans for civil defense were rendered inadequate. Civil defense options once again had to be revamped in the face of this new peril to human life (the presence and danger of fallout were known before the H-bomb blasts, but the power and range of the thermonuclear weapons and their fallout now increased significantly). In conjunction with evacuation and dispersal, fallout shelters now assumed mandatory status in civil defense planning. Even though Ralph Lapp outlined in minute detail "the vertiginous [steep], almost exponential, rise in the hazards faced" as a result of the H-bomb and its fallout, he nevertheless saw progress being made in civil defense as a result of the increased dangers. According to Lapp, in an article originally published in November 1954 in the *Bulletin of Atomic Scientists*, "The year 1954 may well mark the turning point in our C.D. [civil defense] activities. One very favorable index is that more and more top advisors in the government are becoming serious about civil defense. More and more, it is becoming clear that the security of the home base is of paramount importance. In this security, civil defense must assume a high priority."

While Lapp gave reason to hope for a better system of civil defense, he ended his analysis with a warming: "the new peril from radioactive fall-out is more than just a threat to civil defense—it is a peril to humanity." Rather than stressing the need for a strengthened civil defense, the *New Republic* used the information provided by Lapp to question the security guaranteed by anything less than an abandonment of America's nuclear policies and arsenals. Repeating Lapp's prediction that "fifty super-bombs could blanket the entire Northeast USA in a serious-to-lethal radioactive fog," the magazine focused on how "highly vulnerable" the United States therefore was to a Soviet H-bomb attack. A series of challenging questions was posed:

What will be the effect of vulnerability on US policy? Is talk of "massive retaliation" permissible any longer, even as a bluff? Has development of super-weapons already reached the point where their ultimate use is improbable unless a fascination with economizing leaves us so lacking in non-atomic military strength that we would be forced to counter any kind of attack in just one way, by initiating atomic warfare? And must not all of our ingenuity and that of our allies be applied without rest and regardless of setbacks and disappointments to the task of fashioning a formula for atomic disarmament?

The contrary impulses affecting the discussion of civil defense in the era of the hydrogen bomb and radioactive fallout persisted throughout the 1950s. With the development and testing of intercontinental ballistic missiles (ICBMs), the civil defense debate continued divided, with some urging more stringent plans and others doubting the effectiveness of any defense against the swiftly arriving missiles. Some, like President Eisenhower, doubted the overall effectiveness of missiles. Although he supported American programs for missile development, he tried not to rise to the Democratic bait of a "missile gap" [the claim, later proven false, that the Soviets had surpassed the United States in its missile stockpile] in the mid-1950s and he tried to calm fears about Soviet missile progress and the new threat posed by ICBM research and development. In 1956 he bet his life on American safety from Soviet missiles; he registered his certainty in his gambling statement, "I'll wager may life I can sit on any base we've got and in the next ten years the Russians can't hit me with any guided missile." Even though skeptical about missiles, Eisenhower did recognize that missiles carried "a very great psychological value." The continuing debate about civil defense in the late fifties showed the psychological impact of missiles and grew even more extremist after 1957 when the Soviets succeeded both with missiles and with the Sputnik satellite.

Laughing at the Bomb with *Dr. Strangelove*

Paul Boyer

The Cuban Missile Crisis of October 1962 brought the United States and Soviet Union as close to using nuclear weapons against each other as they had ever been before (or ever would be again). Understandably, the idea of nuclear war did not seem much like a laughing matter to most people. All that changed, though, when director Stanley Kubrick released his film *Dr. Strangelove, or How I Learned to Stop Worrying and Love the Bomb* in 1964. A dark comedy that satirized almost all aspects of nuclear culture, Kubrick's film showed the contradictions, dangers, and outright madness of nuclear weapons more clearly than noncomic films like *On the Beach* (1959) or *Fail-Safe* (1964) had. Paul Boyer, Merle Cunti Professor of History and director of the Institute for Research in the Humanities at the University of Wisconsin at Madison, analyzes this film in extensive detail. He describes the process by which Kubrick decided to make a comedy about such a grim topic and explores the extent to which the film is a historically accurate portrayal of the nuclear situation in 1964. Boyer explains some of the real-life figures that Kubrick transformed into the characters of his film, from the insane general Jack D. Ripper to the coldly calculating Dr. Strangelove, after whom the film is named. Boyer also discusses some of the symbolism that Kubrick uses in the film to achieve his scathing criticism of anyone—soldier, politician, diplomat, or scientist—who believed that nuclear weapons were reasonable.

America's top military and civilian leaders gather for an urgent secret session in the nation's capital. An unexpected Cold War crisis threatens to lead to a world-destroying thermonuclear war. A long, rambling message arrives from Moscow, with the Soviet leader alternately blustering indignantly and stammering with fear of what may lie ahead. American strategists solemnly ponder the message: Has the Soviet premier cracked? Is he intoxicated? With humanity's fate hanging in the balance, the hours tick by, and the world edges ever closer to nuclear Armageddon.

This may seem like a scene from Stanley Kubrick's *Dr. Strangelove*, but it really happened. During the October 1962 Cuban Missile Crisis, the White House received a long, almost incoherent message from Nikita Khrushchev, prompting President John F. Kennedy's top decision makers to wonder whether the Soviet leader was drunk. To a greater extent than many might believe, *Dr. Strangelove* faithfully mirrors this historic epoch, in which the world's fate often seemed hostage to accident, miscalculation, and human fallibility.

Of course, *Dr. Strangelove* is not a historical movie in the conventional sense. The precise events it portrays never actually occurred. But this black comedy does have historical resonances. It captures a specific moment and offers a satiric but recognizable portrait of the era's strategic thinking and cultural climate. Its director, Stanley Kubrick, and his co-writers convey all too accurately the weird logic of deterrence theory, the paranoia of the Cold War, and the nuclear jitters of the early 1960s.

Atomic fear, having diminished somewhat from the immediate post-Hiroshima level, increased dramatically after 1954 as hydrogen-bomb tests in the Pacific spread deadly radioactive fallout across parts of North America. While activists demanded a test ban, novelists, magazine editors, science-fiction writers, and moviemakers publicized the threat. Neville Shute's *On the Beach* (1957), made into a bleak 1959 movie by Stanley Kramer, was one product of this apprehension.

Fear intensified during the early 1960s, as President John F. Kennedy, having charged in his 1960 campaign that America faced a "missile gap," approved a nuclear buildup to close it. After sparring with Khrushchev over Berlin in July 1961, Kennedy warned Americans of the dangers of nuclear war and called for an urgent program of fallout-shelter construction. Schoolchildren hid under desks during nuclear drills and, in an animated civil-defense film, learned from Bert the Turtle to "duck and cover." The Cuban Missile Crisis was only the most frightening of a long series of events that made the nuclear threat terrifyingly real. *Dr. Strangelove*, released in January 1964, grew out of this accumulation of nuclear alarms.

Artistic Responses to Real Fears

Dr. Strangelove, however, does more than just reflect the general nuclear anxiety of the time; it also offers insight into the strategic debates of the day. During the 1950s, U.S. policymakers developed deterrence theory as the surest means of avoiding a nuclear war. The fear of massive retaliation, they argued, offered the most credible deterrent to nuclear attack. But how could such a retaliatory threat remain credible if an attacker could destroy the command-and-control centers responsible for launching the counterattack? This dilemma led to studies of automated response systems requiring no human intervention. In *On Thermonuclear War* (1960) and *Thinking about the Unthinkable* (1962), RAND Corporation strategist Herman Kahn coolly discussed (though ultimately rejected) such a strategy. This arcane debate fascinated Kubrick—in 1963, he wrote that he owned "70 or 80 books" on nuclear strategy—and in *Dr. Strangelove* he translated that fascination into black comedy.

Dr. Strangelove was actually one of two 1964 movies that explored the theme of accidental nuclear devastation. The other, *Fail-Safe*, was based on a best-selling 1962 novel by Harvey Wheeler and Eugene Burdick. While *Dr. Strangelove* presented nuclear holocaust as black comedy, *Fail-Safe* played the story straight. Although directed by Sidney Lumet and starring Henry Fonda as the president of the United States, *Fail-Safe* did not capture the public imagination. Instead, it was Kubrick's sardonic version of Armageddon, not Lumet's earnest treatment, that became a classic.

Kubrick, too, based his movie on a recently published novel of Cold War nuclear crisis, Peter George's *Two Hours to Doom* (1958), issued in the United States as *Red Alert*. Up to a point, *Dr. Strangelove* closely follows the plot of George's novel, in which a demented SAC commander orders the 843rd Bomber Wing to launch a nuclear attack on the Soviet Union, unaware that the Russians have deployed an automated retaliation system. But Kubrick made a crucial change in the ending: In *Two Hours to Doom*, the nuclear bomber crashes, and humankind is spared. In the novel's final paragraph, the U.S. president, shaken by the close brush with disaster, pledges to devote the remainder of his term to the search for peace. Kubrick offered no such pat ending or heavy-handed didactic message. Faithful to his darkly comic vision, he grimly followed the ultimate logic of deterrence theory to its horrifying conclusion.

The Plot and Characters

Kubrick portrays a nuclear holocaust arising from the intersection of contemporary nuclear strategy and human fallibility. The action begins as General Jack D. Ripper (Sterling Hayden), in charge of a Strategic Air Command [SAC] unit at Burpelson Air Force Base, launches an unauthorized nuclear attack on Russia. Under the provisions of Wing Attack Plan R, designed as a retaliatory safeguard should Washington be destroyed, only General Ripper has the code necessary to recall the planes. When President Merkin Muffley contacts an inebriated Soviet premier Kissov to warn him of the danger, we learn that the Soviets have built a "doomsday machine." In the event of a U.S. attack, this huge bomb will automatically explode, creating a vast shroud of radioactive fallout that will encircle the earth and kill all life on the planet.

In a brilliant tour de force, the actor Peter Sellers plays a triumvirate of characters: the phlegmatic [apathetic] President Muffley, General Ripper's terrified British aide, Group Captain Lionel Mandrake, and the titular Dr. Strangelove, a former Nazi who changed his name from Unwertigliebe [German for

"Stangelove"] after the war. President Muffley often calls on Strangelove, as the Pentagon's top weapons guru, to explain the intricacies of nuclear strategy. In creating this horribly disabled but ever-smiling character, Kubrick combined parodic elements of Henry Kissinger, the physicist Edward Teller, and the former Nazi rocket scientist Wernher von Braun, each of whom played a central role in U.S. Cold War nuclear policy-making and scientific technology.

Long before he became President Richard Nixon's top foreign-policy adviser, Henry Kissinger had made a reputation for himself as a diplomatic historian and then as a nuclear strategist. His book *A World Restored* (1957) was a scholarly study of Viscount Castlereagh, the conservative [British] statesman who reordered Europe after Napoleon [in the early nineteenth century], and it won him a professorship at Harvard. Turning from history to contemporary strategic issues in *Nuclear Weapons and Foreign Policy* (1957), Kissinger urged the United States to deploy a variety of tactical nuclear weapons to provide additional deterrence in the face of the Soviet threat. In *The Necessity for Choice* (1961), picking up on John Kennedy's 1960 campaign theme, he warned darkly of a growing "missile gap" that invited Soviet expansionism and even nuclear blackmail of the United States.

Edward Teller, a Hungarian Jew who, like Kissinger, fled Europe after Hitler's rise to power, was a brilliant physicist who worked during the war on the Manhattan Project [the top-secret U.S. program that developed the atomic bomb]. While at Los Alamos [the town in New Mexico where the Manhattan Project was headquartered] Teller became convinced of the feasibility of a far more powerful thermonuclear weapon. At California's Lawrence Livermore Laboratory, he oversaw the development and 1952 testing of the first hydrogen bomb. An avid Cold Warrior, he used his considerable influence to push for expansion of America's nuclear arsenal, fiercely opposing the 1963 limited test ban treaty. He also promoted such visionary and controversial schemes to use atomic energy for peacetime purposes as the ill-fated marine engineering scheme, Project Chariot. Teller—whose piercing, deep-set eyes and beetling eyebrows gave him something of the sinister appearance of a stage villain—epitomized the politicized scientists who helped drive the nuclear arms race forward. Antiwar critics recognized his power and in 1970 sardonically presented him with the Dr. Strangelove Award.

Wernher von Braun, blond, blue-eyed, and handsome, was a twenty-one-year-old member of the minor Prussian nobility when Adolf Hitler came to power in 1933. An early rocket enthusiast, the "boy wonder" von Braun became a key technician in the Nazi rocketry program at Peenemünde on the Baltic Sea. Joining the Nazi Party in 1940, he helped persuade Hitler to give the program top priority. In September 1944, the Peenemünde team launched the first V-2 rocket against London. At the war's end, von Braun fled to Bavaria so he could surrender to the Americans rather than to the Russians. Late in 1945 he signed a contract with the U.S. Army. "The next time, I wanted to be on the winning side," he later recalled. By 1950 he was stationed at the army's Redstone Arsenal in Huntsville, Alabama, directing more than a hundred of the German scientists and engineers with whom he had worked in Hitler's day. Von Braun's political flexibility and technocratic approach to missile science inspired a parody by songwriter Tom Lehrer, in which von Braun, in a thick German accent, insists that his job is to launch the missiles, not to worry about where they land: "Dot's not my department, says Wernher von Braun."

The Accuracy of the Film

Is *Dr. Strangelove* historically accurate? In some respects, yes. The information on the U.S. nuclear arsenal and the capability of B-52 bombers is factual. The billboard at Burpelson AFB that proclaims "Peace Is Our Profession" actually adorned some SAC bases. The rantings of General Buck Turgidson (George C. Scott) about "doomsday gaps" and "mine-shaft gaps" directly echo Kennedy's 1960s "missile gap" rhetoric, and Turgidson's description of U.S. casualties in a nuclear war as "get[ting] our hair mussed" caught the lingo of such military men as former SAC commander General Curtis LeMay.

As the near-legendary head of the SAC during the 1950s, the cigar-chomping LeMay provided an easily recognizable archetype for both the grimly fanatical General Ripper and (especially) the bombastic and hyperactive General Turgidson. LeMay never met a bombing plan he didn't like. In 1957 he told two members of the Gaither Commission, which had been formed to assess U.S. military policy, that if a Soviet attack ever seemed likely, he planned to "knock the shit out of them before they got off the ground." Reminded that a preemptive first strike was not U.S. policy, LeMay retorted, "No, it's not national policy, but it's my policy." In 1962, as a member of EXCOM, the top-level team that advised President Kennedy during the Cuban Missile Crisis, LeMay urged a preemptive air strike on missile sites in Cuba, to be followed by an invasion of the island. Retiring from the air force, he ran for vice president in 1968 on a ticket headed by the racist, demagogic governor of Alabama, George C. Wallace. Asked what he would do about the war in Vietnam, LeMay said he would "bomb North Vietnam back into the Stone Age."

Yet the air force angrily challenged the movie's basic premise—an attack order that could not be countermanded. Air force crews in such a situation, insisted the Pentagon, would attack *only* if they received explicit additional instructions confirming the original order. To forestall this official criticism, Kubrick included a notice at the beginning of the film that reads: "IT IS THE STATED POSITION OF THE U.S. AIR FORCE THAT THEIR SAFEGUARDS WOULD PREVENT THE OCCURRENCE OF SUCH EVENTS AS ARE DEPICTED IN THIS FILM." (No doubt surmising that filmgoers' thoughts would quickly turn to the likes of Kissinger, Teller, von Braun, and LeMay, Kubrick's deadpan disclaimer continued: "FURTHERMORE IT SHOULD BE NOTED THAT NONE OF THE CHARACTERS PORTRAYED IN THIS FILM ARE MEANT TO REPRESENT ANY REAL PERSONS LIVING OR DEAD.") But even if *Dr. Strangelove* misrepresented U.S. nuclear command policy for dramatic effect, it accurately captured deepening popular uneasiness about science and technology, as well as growing fears of an arms race escalating out of control. As nuclear stockpiles mounted and intercontinental ballistic missiles (ICBMs) cut attack times from hours to minutes, the potential for catastrophe soared.

The Achievement of Stanley Kubrick

Though an expatriate living in England, Kubrick brilliantly limned U.S. Cold War paranoia. General Ripper, brooding in his claustrophobic office, is a walking embodiment of free-floating cultural fears. Linking his anti-Communist obsessions to his anxieties about the fluoridation of drinking water, Ripper concludes that only a preemptive strike can save America and assure the continued purity of its citizens' "precious bodily fluids." The scenes in which the world's fate hangs on the availability of a dime for a pay phone and President Muffley's ability to reach Omsk Information epitomize both the horror and the absurdity of the nuclear arms race.

Kubrick was also among the first to explore the macho nature of nuclear strategy, a topic much discussed later by psychiatrists and feminists. . . . The movie's title and most of the characters' names suggest a perverse eroticism, and beginning with the celebrated B-52 refueling sequence behind the opening credits (to the tune of "Try a Little Tenderness"), the movie is saturated with sex. General Ripper grips a phallic cigar while pondering his sexual problems. As the holocaust looms, the ever-resourceful Dr. Strangelove describes how the war room elite might survive in deep mine shafts, where it could replenish the human race by copulating nonstop with voluptuous women chosen for their sexual appeal. And in the movie's finale, the B-52 captain played by Slim Pickens mounts a hydrogen bomb as it plummets earthward, waving his cowboy hat in orgiastic ecstasy.

Dr. Strangelove went a long way toward demolishing the traditional war-movie genre. The attack on Burpelson AFB by army troops trying to capture General Ripper is filmed as a grainy newsreel (the entire movie is black-and-white) and staged as a hackneyed combat set piece. Aboard one of the B-52s winging toward Russia, muted drum rolls and the strains of "When Johnny Comes Marching Home Again" echo in the background as Slim Pickens inspires his crew with a cornball homily on the importance of their mission. When the mushroom clouds erupt at last, Vera Lynn croons "We'll Meet Again"—a 1939 song indelibly associated with England's heroic stand during World War II. All of this, of course, is weirdly out of place in the context of global annihilation. It is not only war, suggests Kubrick, but also war movies that will never be the same.

Dr. Strangelove appeared at a transitional moment in America's nuclear history. Nuclear terror, eased by the limited 1963 test ban treaty, diminished still further during the later 1960s and 1970s as arms-control negotiations produced periodic agreements, and as other, temporarily more urgent issues intervened. But as fears revived in the early 1980s, pervasive nuclear anxiety once again produced a cultural fallout of novels, poetry, movies, rock songs, and (something new) television specials that often owed a considerable imaginative debt to Kubrick's pioneering effort. A younger generation rediscovered *Dr. Strangelove* itself.

In the early 1990s, as the nuclear threat eased, the dangers the world had faced in earlier decades loomed even larger in retrospect. Reports of past nuclear accidents and miscalculations surfaced for the first time. Russian and U.S. participants in the 1962 Cuban Missile Crisis gathered to compare notes on their brush with disaster. Simultaneously, revelations from within the former Soviet Union suggested that at one time the Soviets may, in fact, have deployed (or at least developed) an automated retaliatory system—the dreaded "doomsday machine" that is the ultimate deus ex machina of *Dr. Strangelove*. Stanley Kubrick, it now appears, may have cut closer to the truth than even he realized at the time.

The Effect of Nuclear Trauma on Teenagers

John E. Mack

Trauma is a psychiatric term that is used to describe a state of shock that a person goes into after a severe physical or emotional strain such as a car accident. In this article, John E. Mack, former professor of psychiatry, Cambridge Hospital of Harvard Medical School, discusses the results of a survey given to a thousand teenagers from 1978 to 1980 to measure whether their responses demonstrate a kind of trauma caused by growing up with anxieties about nuclear war. Mack first lists a number of representative responses that the researchers received to their questions about nuclear weapons and nuclear war. He then interprets these responses from the perspective of a clinical psychiatrist, highlighting patterns of fear, bitterness, and helplessness that are typical of patients suffering from trauma. His conclusion is that the daily stress of being forced to consider the potential destruction of their world has created deep emotional distress in many of these teenagers and that this distress frequently causes substantial problems in their development into adults. Perhaps ironically, the students that Mack and his collaborators interviewed grew up during what was arguably the most peaceful era of the Cold War, the decade and a half of détente that existed between the superpowers from the mid-1960s to the late 1970s. Nevertheless, Mack illustrates that they show signs of being deeply disturbed by the prospects of a nuclear war occurring in their lifetimes.

John E. Mack, "Psychosocial Trauma," *The Final Epidemic: Physicians and Scientists on Nuclear War,* edited by Ruth Adams and Susan Cullen. Chicago, IL: Educational Foundation for Nuclear Science, 1981. Copyright © 1981 by the Educational Foundation for Nuclear Science, Inc. All rights reserved. Reproduced by permission.

A questionnaire was given to 1,000 grammar and high school students between 1978 and 1980. More detailed responses were obtained from 100 students (10th to 12th grades) in the Boston area who were attending two schools, one a public school about 30 miles north of Boston, the other a private school 10 miles west of the city. The students were asked such questions as "What does the word nuclear bring to mind?" "How old were you when you were first aware of nuclear advances [i.e., developments in nuclear weapon technology]?" "Have you participated in any activity related to nuclear technology?" "Do you think you could survive a nuclear attack?" "Have nuclear advances influenced your plans for marriage, having children or planning for the future?" and "Have nuclear advances affected your way of thinking about the future, your view of the world, and time?" We were aware that the use of the word "advances" is in one sense euphemistic, reflecting a kind of obliqueness of approach to a topic which includes the production of weapons that threaten human annihilation.

The students given the questionnaires probably represent a somewhat biased sample, as they are better informed about the dangers of nuclear war than we would expect the average adolescent school population to be (whatever may be meant by "average"). The comments are, nevertheless, quite disturbing and demonstrate that the imminent threat of nuclear annihilation has penetrated deeply into their consciousness. Some of their responses are as follows:

What does the word nuclear bring to mind?

"Danger, death, sadness, corruption, explosion, cancer, children, waste, bombs, pollution, terrible, terrible devaluing of human life."

"Nuclear means a source of energy which could provide the world with energy needed for future generations. It also means the destruction of marine life whose environment is ruined by nuclear waste. Also the destruction of human life when used in missiles."

The great majority did not believe that they, their city or the country could survive a nuclear attack.

The comments below are characteristic of the ones received in response to the question.

Have nuclear advances influenced your plans for marriage, having children or planning for the future?

"I don't choose to bring up children in a world of such horrors and dangers of deformation. The world might be gone in two seconds from now, but I still plan for the future, because I am going to live as long as I am going to live."

"Nuclear advances are not always on my mind. My philosophy is that life is full of dangers and troubles and worries—I can't spend my time on earth a psychologically sick person, afraid that at any moment I will die. I feel that I would refrain from having children, though, not because of thermonuclear threats—because I am not crazy about children."

"No, not really because if there is a nuclear war there is no sense in worrying about it because whatever happens will happen. The technology is there and it can destroy the world."

Have nuclear advances affected your way of thinking about the future, your view of the world, and time?

"I am constantly aware that at any second the world might blow up in my face. It makes living more interesting."

"I don't really worry about it, but it is terrifying to think that the world may not be here in a half hour. But I am still going to live for now."

"I am strongly against it because the people who are in control of it are not worth trusting the whole world in their hands! It's much too much power for one person to hold."

"I think that, unless we do something about nuclear weapons the world and the human race may not have much time left (corny, huh?)."

"It gives me a pretty dim view of the world and mankind but it hasn't really influenced me."

"Everything has to be looked at on two levels: The world with the threat of ending soon, and life with future, etc. The former has to be blocked out for everyday functioning because very few people can find justification for living otherwise. But

Many Americans in the late 1950s and early 1960s built back-yard fallout shelters in the hopes of surviving a nuclear attack.

[it] is always there—on a much larger scale than possibilities of individual deaths, car accidents, etc.—even though the result to me personally would be the same."

"Yes, probably a little. It makes you wonder about how anyone could even dare to hurt others so badly."

"Quite definitely, I believe that we should try to save ourselves; any form of suicide alters the future. It would end our race."

"I sincerely hope that we stay on good terms with the USSR. I hope they never consider a nuclear war."

"I feel our growth is speeding up and if we don't slow down then we're going to die. These advances are too quick and they seem to be taking over our world."

"I feel that everyone's views of the world and ideas of the future have changed somewhat. I feel that the future is very unsettled and a nuclear war could destroy the world in a short time."

"I think that a nuclear war, which could break out in a relatively short period of time in the far future, could nearly destroy the world."

"In a way it has. It has shown me how stupid some adults can be. If they know it could easily kill them I have no idea why they support it. Once in a while it makes me start to think that the end of my time in life may not be as far off as I would like it to be."

"Yes, I feel if men keep going on with experiments they are bound to make one mistake that could mean the end of a lot of surrounding cities and if severe enough the end of what we know today as the world."

Interpreting the Responses

The questionnaires showed that these adolescents are deeply disturbed by the threat of nuclear war, have doubt about the future and about their own survival. There is a revelation in these responses of the experience of fear and menace. There is also cynicism, sadness, bitterness and a sense of helplessness. They feel unprotected. Some have doubts about planning families or are unable to think ahead in any long-term sense.

We may be seeing that growing up in a world dominated by the threat of imminent nuclear destruction is having an impact on the structure of personality itself. It is difficult, however, to separate the impact of the threat of nuclear war from other factors in contemporary culture, such as the relentless confrontation of adolescents by the mass media with a deluge of social and political problems which their parents' generation seems helpless to change.

It seems that these young people are growing up without the ability to form stable ideals, or the sense of continuity upon which the development of stable personality structure and the formation of serviceable ideals depend. We may find we are raising generations of young people without a basis for making long-term commitments, who are given over, of necessity, to doctrines of impulsiveness and immediacy in their personal relationships or choice of behaviors and activity. At the very least these young people need an opportunity to learn about and participate in decisions on matters which affect their lives so critically.

The experience of powerlessness of children and adolescents, the sense they have that matters are out of control, is not different from the way most adults feel in relation to the nuclear arms race. Little can be done to help our young people unless adults address the apathy and helplessness that we experience in relation to the arms race and the threat of nuclear war.

The Day After
Brings Nuclear War
to Television

Jay Cocks

The nuclear anxieties of the early 1980s were at their high point late in 1983 when the ABC television network broadcast *The Day After*, the first made-for-television movie to depict the effects of a nuclear war. Although the film was not well received artistically—this review by *Time* magazine correspondent Jay Cocks is not alone in panning its storytelling—it further stimulated a public debate about the continuing risks associated with nuclear weapons. This article, published a month before *The Day After* aired, discusses the cultural context that surrounded the release of the film. Antinuclear activists hailed it as a powerful fictional demonstration of the perils that nuclear weapons promised. On the other hand, detractors claimed that the film distorted political realities and offered a defeatist view of how well policies of nuclear deterrence had actually helped prevent nuclear war. The filmmakers distanced themselves from either side, claiming that the film's purpose was simply to depict what a nuclear war and its aftermath might look like. Several million viewers tuned in to watch the film when it eventually aired, and public reaction was mixed. Artistic merit aside, *The Day After* turned out to be one of the most widely seen responses to the difficulties of living under the threat of nuclear war and, as the

Jay Cocks, "The Nightmare Comes Home," *Time*, vol. 122, October 24, 1983, pp. 84–86. Copyright © 1983 by Time, Inc. Reproduced by permission.

end of this article implies, spawned a number of similar film projects in its wake.

Peanuts. Or so says a desperate, despairing physician in *The Day After*. Even Hiroshima was peanuts compared with the irrevocable thermonuclear slaughter visited on Kansas City and its environs. Lawrence. Sedalia. Green Ridge. They have all been devastated. But this is not some horrible, local nuclear accident. This is worldwide atomic warfare. The missiles have been launched, the bombs have gone off. The global village has been nuked.

No escape, no hope. And no happy endings either. Only the suggestion of a blighted tomorrow, full of radiation poisoning that desiccates survivors and deforms unborn children. Say this for *The Day After*: it has no patience for reassurance and makes no kind of political peace. It sets itself a relatively easy mark—to illustrate the ravages of nuclear war—but a punishingly high goal. It may be that no television film has ever had such ambition, or presumption, and just so no one misses the point, the network and the film makers spell it out in grave white letters just before the final fade: "It is hoped that the images of this film will inspire the nations of this earth, their people and leaders, to find the means to avert the fateful day."

The Day After will not be broadcast until Nov. 20 [1983], but its political implications have already been discussed, denounced and championed by proponents and opponents of the nuclear freeze. ABC executives are united and adamant about the apolitical nature of their 2-hr. 5-min. presentation. "We never intended the film to be a political statement," claims Brandon Stoddard, president of ABC Motion Pictures and the initiator of the project. "The movie simply says that nuclear war is horrible. That is all it says. That is a very safe statement." Adds the film's director, Nicholas Meyer: "*The Day After* does not advocate disarmament, build-down, buildup, freeze. I didn't want to alienate any viewers. The movie is like a giant public service announcement, like Smokey the Bear."

The movie has already started its fair share of brush fires. Tape copies leaked into circulation and were being screened for freeze sympathizers as long ago as July. Congressman Edward Markey, co-sponsor of a House freeze resolution, caught an early show and says, "It's the most important television program ever because it's the most important issue ever. It's the most honest account of nuclear war that has been done." "It's an awesome film," adds Congressman Thomas J. Downey. For Janet Michaud, executive director of the Campaign Against Nuclear War, "ABC is performing an enormous public service. It's giving the American people the ability to become part of the debate over the most important issue of our times." For Roger Molander, founder of the nuclear-war-education group Ground Zero, *The Day After* is a conduit to confrontation. "To come to grips with the reality of nuclear war, one has to go through a nuclear passage, to confront a nuclear war in all its horror. This will provide a passage for 30, 40, 50 million Americans."

Television networks, which like to hear numbers like that, nevertheless give a collective corporate shudder at the slightest hint of advocacy. "ABC's responsibility is to the film itself," says Stoddard. "How it is perceived or used by other people is beyond our control." That may be, but the freeze supporters have made a strong head start. Leaked copies of *The Day After* are being shown at antinuke fund raisers, while the opposition has been effectively shut out. "This film has been used to generate interest and support, including financial support, for our efforts," Michaud admits.

Paul Dietrich, president of the conservative National Center for Legislative Research, wangled himself an invitation to a private showing and calls the film "anything but non-partisan." Says John Fisher, president of the American Security Council: "Clearly someone associated with the production has a significantly different perspective than we do, because somehow the pirated version hasn't been exposed to people on our side of the issue. This movie says deterrence has failed, and that's a political statement."

Having made the film their own, freeze advocates are now using it, in the words of Disarmament Activist Josh Baran, "to educate people. It is the best use of television I can think of."

Last April, Baran helped start an *ad hoc* organization called The Day Before, which will work with 17 national antinuclear groups to set up seminars in more than 100 cities around the country for two days following the film's air date. Ground Zero will mail out 100,000 viewing guides. The Center for Defense Information is considering producing a 60-sec. commercial, narrated by Paul Newman, offering "a nuclear war-prevention kit." "I plan to send in for one of those kits," writes Conservative Columnist William F. Buckley Jr., "and if Mr. Newman doesn't send me an MX missile, I'm going to report him to the Postal Service people for fraud."

All this heat and dust have made advertisers, already shy of buying time on such a dubiously commercial program as *The Day After*, almost paralyzed with reluctance. By some accounts, the network has lined up four or five sponsors; by others, it has sold only half the 25 available 30-sec. commercial spots. "I couldn't confirm half, but I know it's a good portion," comments Jeff Tolvin, ABC's director of business information, with gingerly care. The network is charging a hefty $135,000 a spot —a price that could dip as show time approaches and empty air time looms—but the problem, according to Madison Avenue, is not monetary. "It may be one of the most devastating pieces of film I've ever seen, TV or otherwise, but it is artistically unsuitable to most of our clients," says Joel Segal, senior vice president of broadcasting for Ted Bates Advertising. "It isn't the issue of controversy; it's more a matter of the commercials' conflicting grossly with the content of the program." Asks another agency executive: "Do you want singing and dancing and music in that kind of program environment?"

The scenario is not too elaborate or cynical for the byzantine world of show biz: sponsor recalcitrance triggers stress. Tapes are leaked, positions taken, battle lines drawn, articles written. No movie since CBS's 1980 Holocaust film *Playing for Time* has stirred such a dust devil of ideological p.r. [public relations], but the stakes are even larger here. *The Day After* cost an opulent $7 million, and its promotion budget may ultimately equal that figure. ABC, gambling that it will make up in ratings what it misses in ad dollars, schedules the film for sweeps week, when the three networks all go for broke in the ratings. The timing is perfect: Nov. 20 is not only a Nielsen trifecta, it is less than two weeks before the Pershing IIs [nuclear missiles] are due to be installed in West Germany. More controversy, more publicity. Is the timing a reflection of political intent as well as business expediency? The network firmly denies it. The *National Review* editorializes that ABC is making "a $7 million contribution to the faltering campaign against the deployment of the Pershing II." So *The Day After* lumbers in carting more weight than Mother Courage [allegorical character in a play by German dramatist Bertolt Brecht].

For all this, the film's beginnings were astonishingly humble: Brandon Stoddard saw *The China Syndrome* [a film about an accident at a nuclear power plant] and wondered what the home-front consequences of nuclear war would be. When Nicholas Meyer met Jason Robards on an airplane and offered him the lead role of a humanistic surgeon, Robards accepted with elegant simplicity. "It beats signing petitions," he said. Now that *The Day After* has been temporarily positioned right at the center of the nuclear debate, there is no more room for humility or modesty. The finished film was premiered last week in Lawrence, Kans., where much of it had been made on location, and the townspeople were tearful and shaken. Stoddard reports he wept when he saw the first cut of the film and says the present version "is the most important thing I have ever done." Director Meyer calls the movie "the most valuable thing I've ever done with my life." Mayor David Longhurst has invited Ronald Reagan and Yuri Andropov to Lawrence for a summit. Another Lawrence citizen, Bob Swan, member of the antinuke Let Lawrence Live organization, says he is trying to link up his home town by television or telephone to Leningrad, so that Soviets and Americans can hash things out person to person. After the broadcast, ABC will put on a special 45-min. edition of *Viewpoint*, anchored by Ted Koppel. The show, intended as both a kind of emotional decompression chamber for viewers and a debating platform between friends and foes of the freeze, has an additional, and certainly not accidental, function. It gives *The Day After* the weight of a major news event.

Nothing, however, can give it the substance. Under all the furor, spontaneous or manufactured, and the high urgency, real or prefabricated just for the premiere, is the film, a frail vessel indeed to bear the fate of mankind. History and distance have not made Stanley Kubrick's 1964 film *Dr. Strangelove* any less great or—sadly—less relevant, but even a movie as fine as that would have to struggle to stay above the sort of ideological tide surging around *The Day After*. No one has yet made the case that *Dr. Strangelove* has been bested, although there are suggestions, even from Meyer, that it has been beaten out in the high earnestness sweepstakes. Meyer concedes his movie "has a minimum of imagination" but thinks *Dr. Strangelove* is "distilled through comedy," which presumably means that his own enterprise, being so conspicuously short of humor, serves some loftier social purpose. This type of cultural con is a piece of undiluted show-biz self-protection, and a good thing too. Political immediacy is just about all *The Day After* has going for it. By any standards other than social, it is a terrible movie.

The film is so aimlessly anecdotal in its opening positions that there is little dramatic connection between the characters. Reality is so quickly and cursorily observed that there seems nothing else to do but bring on the bombs. There are no people here, only targets, stick figures on a Midwestern landscape waiting to be wasted. A kind of predictable character collage revolving erratically around the travails of Robards' nicely realized surgeon, the movie misses dramatic force because it has no center. It does, however, have a centerpiece, a 4-min. sequence representing the atomization of Middle America and, by extension, much of the rest of the world.

People turn where they stand into living X rays just before they disintegrate entirely. Fire storms swallow up towns. The images of destruction, mild for a theatrical movie and practically gentle by any factual measure, are still startling by American television standards, and they pack force. Once this montage of immediate death ends, however, *The Day After* has to get back to its characters, which is to say that it must run on empty. Nuclear annihilation may be the subject, but the film appears to have been the victim of an editorial chain-saw massacre.

Whatever the executive reasons for reducing its three-hour running time to just over two may have been, considerations of dramatic coherence cannot have numbered high among them. The female lead (Jobeth Williams) dies off-screen, her passing noted in just a line or two of dialogue. Another major character, a farmer and family man (John Cullum), gets shot by squatters, and his widowed wife and orphaned children react only by turning toward the sound of the gun. Characters tumble in and out like cards in a dropped deck.

Paradoxically, when the film is vaguest it is often at its strongest. Impending nuclear war is announced in a series of bulletins on radio and television, casually broadcast and half-heard at first. The sound track carries snatches of references that accelerate to slightly longer descriptions of airport blockades and MiG-25s [Soviet fighter planes] "invading West German airspace" and that end, finally, with a shocked anchorwoman saying, "Three nuclear weapons in the low-kiloton range were airburst this morning over advancing Soviet troops." There is only calamity after that. ABC's determination to keep up appearances of political evenhandedness have helped the film makers conjure up what seems like a spookily accurate scenario for Armageddon: the beginnings of worldwide disaster as a series of barely overheard fragments. This is global tragedy with no fixed responsibility.

Screenwriter Edward Hume and the film makers were correct in choosing to avoid blaming either the U.S. or the U.S.S.R. for the initiation of catastrophe. This moral neutrality may be one reason the network is actually going to broadcast their film, advertisers or not, champions or not, critics or not. Less than 20 years ago, the BBC refused to show Peter Watkins' very similar but far more devastating *The War Game* because it was "too horrifying." *The Day After*, nowhere near as strong or as skillful, is still frightening enough, and here it is, occupying more than two hours of prime commercial network time. But such a signal of cultural change can also be an intimation of trouble. The generally shabby quality of *The Day After* is of major concern because, rather than startling audiences into a new awareness, it is just as likely to anesthetize them with mediocrity.

This process will not stop with *The Day After*. Paramount already has movie in the pipeline called *Testament*, about one family trying to survive a nuclear blast. One of the hottest commercial novels due next spring is *Warday* by Whitley Strieber and James Kunetka, which shows America reeling from atomic desolation and California, intact and safe, effectively closed to the rest of the country. "There's a hell of a percentage increase in these day-after nuclear scripts," says Michael Fuchs, president of Home Box Office's entertainment group. Apocalypse has clearly become something more than the fate that looms just over the horizon line. It may be the growth industry of the '80s.

CHAPTER 3

Voices of Protest

The United States Should Share the Secret of the Bomb

Freda Kirchwey

Freda Kirchwey was a liberal activist and the editor and publisher of the *Nation*, a liberal journal of opinion, from 1937 to 1955. In this editorial, published just more than three months after the use of atomic bombs on the Japanese cities of Hiroshima and Nagasaki, Kirchwey makes the argument that keeping the secret of the atomic bomb from the U.S. wartime Allies—especially the Soviet Union (which she calls "Russia" throughout this article)—is a recipe for disaster that will eventually lead to nuclear war. In stating this view, Kirchwey joined with a number of other prominent figures, including several of the scientists who worked on the Manhattan Project and members of President Truman's cabinet. Kirchwey argues that remaining secretive about the atomic bomb only creates suspicion and fear among the Soviets about American motives. She contends that giving Russia the secret of the bomb—which she claims (rightly, as it turned out) they and other nations are likely to discover in due course anyway—will stop an arms race before it begins and allow the nations of the world to focus on the rebuilding process in the aftermath of World War II. She also argues that giving up the secret would obligate the Soviets to participate in international control of atomic energy as part of the newly formed United Nations, thereby contributing to the peace and stability of the postwar

Freda Kirchwey, "Russia and the Bomb," *The Nation*, vol. 161, November 17, 1945, pp. 511–12.

world. President Truman chose not to adopt the view of Kirchwey and those like her, and the remainder of his presidency was marked by a rapidly growing hostility between the United States and the Soviet Union, both of which possessed nuclear weapons by the time he left office in 1952.

That Russia should be given full information about the atomic bomb is so evident that the question no longer seems arguable. The obvious objections have been answered with devastating finality in the last few weeks [fall of 1945] by many scientists and a few public men. They have proved beyond question that not even the narrowest concept of national security will be served by secrecy. Since this is so, the longer the matter is discussed the worse for all of us, for the debate itself generates poisons out of which, if they are not soon neutralized and washed away, the next war—the Atomic War— will certainly come.

Our secrecy policy, restated only the other day by President [Harry] Truman, would have been accepted without question in other circumstances. A new weapon of ordinary dimensions, according to traditional practices, is kept for the use of the country that perfects it; only in the course of actual warfare would the secret be shared even with a trusted ally. The war was over almost immediately after the bombs hit Hiroshima and Nagasaki. And nothing that has happened since then has increased official American or British trust in our Russian ally. What more natural, therefore, than to sit tight on the secret of the bomb, particularly in view of its unprecedented destructive power?

Natural, but futile, and therefore stupid. For the destructive power of atomic explosion is exactly what makes an attempt to monopolize it more dangerous than the bomb itself. It is not merely a new weapon. It is a weapon which gives the nation controlling it the power of life or death over any other nation. This is a situation which in its essence is intolerable. At the same time, as the nuclear scientists have patiently explained, it is a situation impossible to perpetuate. Put those two facts together in proper proportions and you have the makings of the greatest explosion on earth.

Foreign Reaction to the U.S. Nuclear Monopoly

Many people, I believe, were temporarily deceived by the restraint exhibited by other nations in discussing America's monopoly on total destruction. It seemed at first as if our allies, grateful for the sudden ending of hostilities and awed by our overpowering display of energy, creative ability, and cold cash, were prepared to accept us as the appointed trustees on earth of the released power of the universe. Even Russia said not a word. But soon, very soon, the reaction began, and it has been growing steadily in many parts of the world; its most important manifestation has been a solid, total deadlock in our relations with Russia. It is that deadlock which strangled the Foreign Ministers' conference in London [in September 1945] and kept Russia out of the [October 1945] meeting of the Far Eastern advisory commission in Washington. It is that deadlock which has brought [British] Prime Minister [Clement] Attlee to the White House.

But what of it?, some of the arguers may still ask. Suppose Russia doesn't like it, what then? Didn't [former British Prime Minister Winston] Churchill have the answer when he said that even during the war Russia had shown little inclination to share its military secrets with its allies, and would hardly hand over the secret of the bomb today if it had it? This position might be worth considering—though at best it betrays a rather juvenile approach to a grimly adult problem—if the United States were permitted the freedom to decide which Mr. Churchill and Mr. Truman and most of our military leaders assume for purposes of debate. The scientists have ruthlessly snatched away that freedom. We can't keep the secret because every advanced nation already knows all we know about atomic energy and how to release it, and even our last reserved area, the sacred American "know-how," will be conquered soon.

This is accepted fact; neither General [George] Marshall [secretary of state at the time] nor Mr. Truman would think of disputing it. What, then, do they hope to gain by hiding our technical knowledge behind barred gates and building stockpiles of hatred and suspicion abroad? What do they hope to gain by legislation creating a federal dictatorship over all atomic investigation, as well as production, and making the interchange of scientific information in the field of nuclear experiment impossible under threat of criminal prosecution? What is it all about, if Russia and Sweden and France, and perhaps Spain and Argentina, will be able to make bombs within the next five years?

Motives for Keeping the Atomic Secret

The answer is a complex one. Chiefly, they hope to gain time. And in the time gained, they hope to do two incompatible things: first, accumulate a lot of improved atomic bombs so that we can maintain our head-start in destructive power; and, second, create some sort of international control to take charge of the situation when other nations finally get around to manufacturing bombs themselves. This sounds, perhaps, too silly to be taken seriously, but it is the only explanation so far publicly offered for our policy of secrecy. If you suggest that secrecy plus bomb-production makes difficult the achievement of that mutual trust—especially with Russia—on which any effective international control must rest, you will be fobbed off with the theme that ran through Mr. Truman's unfortunate Navy Day speech: The bomb is a sacred trust; everyone in the world believes us and knows that we will not violate that trust. The only catch is that the premise is inaccurate. How inaccurate, can be best realized if for a moment one imagines that Russia possesses the secret of the bomb and has announced in the same pious words its determination to hang on to it. Would we decide forthwith to drop our efforts to make a bomb of our own? Would we accept Russia's protestations of good will? The questions answer themselves, and demolish at the same time the position of those who hope to build a structure of international trust on a foundation of Anglo-American (though chiefly American) monopoly of atomic power.

Only one explanation of our policy would make sense. A short period of secrecy would be worth the cost if we intended to start an offensive war against Russia or if we expected Russia to attack us in the immediate future. In either case our temporary monopoly would give us an overwhelming advantage; we could destroy Russian cities and industries without fear of retaliation and quickly bring the Soviet Union to total defeat. But this, the one sensible explanation for our present policy, paradoxically makes no sense whatever. For in spite of our bluster and our camouflaged designs on strategic bases, and our shocked objections to other nations' similar designs; in spite of a few generals and Congressmen and newspaper editors who, accepting war with Russia as inevitable, argue with a sort of maniac's logic that it had best come soon while we have the upper hand; in spite of all this, the United States is not going to attack Russia. And Russia is not going to attack us, bomb or no bomb. One can be certain that no disagreements Moscow may have with any major power will be allowed to develop to the point of war as long as Russia is desperately struggling to restore its shattered economic life and rebuild its cities. The Soviet Union needs peace even more than we do.

The Potential Dangers of the Secret

In fact the reality is exactly the opposite and the danger a very different one. Since the chance of our being involved in war in the next two or three years is remote, the possession of the bomb-secret is a positive disadvantage and the bomb becomes a weapon aimed at ourselves. If we don't intend to use it first, we are creating suspicion without any compensating benefit. By the time other nations have made bombs of their own, the international situation may have so deteriorated as to make certain a war in which we shall be the attacked, not the attacker, and our guarded secret, our "sacred trust," will ironically have been one of the chief factors in producing the breakdown.

The position I have put here is not only supported by most liberal opinion in America; the British press, from left to right, accepts as a prerequisite to all further international action the necessity for conquering Russia's distrust by giving it the secret of the bomb. Presumably the Prime Minister will convey to the President that point of view and the various reasons for it.

He must persuade Mr. Truman that those advisers are wrong who recently urged that Russia should not be let in on the secret "until the various peace settlemets have been finally determined." Their insistence that the bomb gives the United States and Britain "dominance in current discussions" has been disproved by events. The contrary is the case. Only if we approach Russia with the secret (not the bomb) in one hand and our proposals in the other will the proposals be taken at their face value. At present they make a funny noise when we drop them on the conference table.

The Benefits of Atomic Openness

A decision to give the bomb to Russia would immediately shift to new ground the other urgent problems facing the powers. It would not solve those problems. The differences between Russia and the West are real differences; they existed long before the first bomb was dropped and they would still exist if Russia had the secret. But the bomb has intensified them and stalled efforts to solve them. [Russian foreign minister Vyacheslav] Molotov opened the way to a new attempt to overcome those differences in his speech last week. He stated clearly but moderately Russia's intention to develop the bomb through its own efforts, he offered a detailed explanation of Russian policy, domestic and foreign, and he emphasized the desire of the government for close cooperation among the Big Three. "Expressions of good intentions are not enough," he said. "The Soviet Union has been and will continue to be a reliable bulwark in the defense of peace and the security of peoples, and is ready to prove this not in words but in deeds."

If Attlee and Truman want to put Molotov's promise to the test, they can easily do so. The bomb is not a bargaining counter to be used to extract from Russia concessions which would serve the national interests of Britain and the United States. It must be given freely. But in giving it, the Western powers would have a right to assure themselves and the world that Russia will accept genuine international control of atomic power and will cooperate in converting the machinery of peace to the demands of the new age. Much needs to be done to the structure of the United Nations Organization and to the rules under which it operates before it can be trusted with powers of atomic control. Russia must be ready to accept such chances, as must the Western powers themselves.

If the necessity to give Russia the secret of the bomb is self-evident, there are subsidiary questions of vast importance that require detailed consideration. Many dangers could be avoided if the conferees in Washington would settle the secrecy issue quickly and get on to those other matters. For the secret is only an obstacle; the real problems lie on the other side.

World Government Can Prevent Nuclear War

Albert Einstein

Albert Einstein is perhaps the most important scientist of the twentieth century. His theory of relativity revolutionized the study of physics and changed the basic conception of the universe as much as any scientific concept since Copernicus and Galileo proved that the earth revolved around the sun. He also played an important role in the development of atomic weapons, not only because his theories contributed greatly to the knowledge needed to release energy from within atoms, but also because of a letter he wrote to President Franklin Roosevelt in 1939. Einstein became convinced that scientists in Nazi Germany had begun working to create an atomic bomb, and he urged Roosevelt to start a similar program to prevent the Nazis from being either the first or the only possessors of such a potentially destructive weapon. In large part due to Einstein's insistence, Roosevelt established the Manhattan Project in 1941, which eventually created the bombs that Truman would use against Japan in 1945.

After being horrified by the effects of the bomb's use at Hiroshima and Nagasaki, Einstein became a leading advocate for the strict international control of nuclear weapons. He eventually expanded this idea into a proposal for a comprehensive world government that would move beyond the limited, if also unprecedented, power that had been given to the United Nations after World War II. In this article from November 1947 Einstein expresses his belief that none of the policies adopted toward nuclear weapons since 1945 by any country had helped ensure that a nuclear war would not happen. In fact, he argues that such a war had become more likely, a situation he finds morally unacceptable because of its potential for massive destruction. Einstein lists what he considers to be shortsighted actions on the part of both the United States and the Soviet Union and claims that the risk of nuclear war will diminish only when both sides agree to entrust the task of ensuring peace to a world government that represents the interests of all nations, not just those with the most technologically advanced weapons.

Since the completion of the first atomic bomb [in July 1945] nothing has been accomplished to make the world more safe from war, while much has been done to increase the destructiveness of war. I am not able to speak from any firsthand knowledge about the development of the atomic bomb, since I do not work in this field. But enough has been said by those who do to indicate that the bomb has been made more effective. Certainly the possibility can be envisaged of building a bomb of far greater size, capable of producing destruction over a larger area. It also is credible that an extensive use could be made of radioactivated gases which would spread over a wide region, causing heavy loss of life without damage to buildings.

I do not believe it is necessary to go on beyond these possibilities to contemplate a vast extension of bacteriological warfare. I am skeptical that this form presents dangers comparable with those of atomic warfare. Nor do I take into account a danger of starting a chain reaction of a scope great enough to destroy part or all of this planet. I dismiss this on the ground that if it could happen from a man-made atomic explosion it would already have happened from the action of the cosmic rays which are continually reaching the earth's surface.

But it is not necessary to imagine the earth being destroyed like a nova by a stellar explosion to understand vividly the growing scope of atomic war and to recognize that unless another war is prevented it is likely to bring destruction on a scale never before held possible and even now hardly conceived, and that little civilization would survive it.

No Preventive Steps Have Been Taken

In the first two years of the atomic era [1945–1947] another phenomenon is to be noted. The public, having been warned of the horrible nature of atomic warfare, has done nothing about it, and to a large extent has dismissed the warning from its consciousness. A danger that cannot be averted had perhaps better be forgotten; or a danger against which every possible precaution has been taken also had probably better be forgotten. That is, if the United States had dispersed its industries and decentralized its cities, it might be reasonable for people to forget the peril they face.

I should say parenthetically that it is well that this country has not taken these precautions, for to have done so would make atomic war still more probable, since it would convince the rest of the world that we are resigned to it and are preparing for it. But nothing has been done to avert war, while much has been done to make atomic war more horrible; so there is no excuse for ignoring the danger.

I say that nothing has been done to avert war since the completion of the atomic bomb, despite the proposal for supranational [that is, beyond the level of a single nation] control [the Baruch Plan, which was subsequently rejected] of atomic energy put forward by the United States in the United Nations. This country has made only a conditional proposal, and on conditions which the Soviet Union is now determined not to accept. This makes it possible to blame the failure on the Russians.

But in blaming the Russians the Americans should not ignore the fact that they themselves have not voluntarily renounced the use of the bomb as an ordinary weapon in the time before the achievement of supranational control, or if supranational control is not achieved. Thus they have fed the fear of other countries that they consider the bomb a legitimate part of their arsenal so long as other countries decline to accept their terms for supranational control.

Americans may be convinced of their determination not to launch an aggressive or preventive war. So they may believe it is superfluous to announce publicly that they will not a second time be the first to use the atomic bomb. But this country has been solemnly invited to renounce the use of the bomb—that is, to outlaw it—and has declined to do so unless its terms for supranational control are accepted.

The Problem with American Nuclear Policy

I believe this policy is a mistake. I see a certain military gain from not renouncing the use of the bomb in that this may be deemed to restrain another country from starting a war in which the United States might use it. But what is gained in one way is lost in another. For an understanding over the supranational control of atomic energy has been made more remote. That may be no military drawback so long as the United States has the exclusive use of the bomb. But the moment another country is able to make it in substantial quantities, the United States loses greatly through the absence of an international agreement, because of the vulnerability of its concentrated industries and its highly developed urban life.

In refusing to outlaw the bomb while having the monopoly of it, this country suffers in another respect, in that it fails to return publicly to the ethical standards of warfare formally accepted previous to the last war. It should not be forgotten that the atomic bomb was made in this country as a preventive measure; it was to head off its use by the Germans, if they discovered it. The bombing of civilian centers was initiated by the Germans and adopted by the Japanese. To it the Allies responded in kind—as it turned out, with greater effectiveness— and they were morally justified in doing so. But now, without any provocation, and without the justification of reprisal or retaliation, a refusal to outlaw the use of the bomb save in reprisal is making a political purpose of its possession. This is hardly pardonable.

I am not saying that the United States should not manufacture and stockpile the bomb, for I believe that it must do so; it must be able to deter another nation from making an atomic attack when it also has the bomb. But deterrence should be the only purpose of the stockpile of bombs. In the same way I believe that the United Nations should have the atomic bomb when it is supplied with its own armed forces and weapons. But it too should have the bomb for the sole purpose of deterring an aggressor or rebellious nations from making an atomic attack. It should not use the atomic bomb on its own initiative any more than the United States or any other power should do so. To keep a stockpile of atomic bombs without promising not to initiate its use is exploiting the possession of the bombs for political ends. It may be that the United States hopes in this way to frighten the Soviet Union into accepting supranational control of atomic energy. But the creation of fear only heightens antagonism and increases the danger of war. I am of the opinion that this policy has detracted from the very real virtue in the offer of supranational control of atomic energy.

The Bad Ethics of the Cold War

We have emerged from a war in which we had to accept the degradingly low ethical standards of the enemy. But instead of feeling liberated from his standards, and set free to restore the sanctity of human life and the safety of noncombatants, we are in effect making the low standards of the enemy in the last war our own for the present. Thus we are starting toward another war degraded by our own choice.

It may be that the public is not fully aware that in another war atomic bombs will be available in large quantities. It may measure the dangers in the terms of the three bombs exploded before the end of the last war. The public also may not appreciate that, in relation to the damage inflicted, atomic bombs already have become the most economical form of destruction that can be used on the offensive. In another war the bombs will be plentiful and they will be comparatively cheap. Unless there is a determination not to use them that is far stronger than can be noted today among American political and military leaders, and on the part of the public itself, atomic warfare will be hard to avoid. Unless Americans come to recognize that they are not stronger in the world because they have the bomb, but weaker because of their vulnerability to atomic attack, they are not likely to conduct their policy at Lake Success or in their relations with Russia in a spirit that furthers the arrival at an understanding.

The Russians Share the Blame

But I do not suggest that the American failure to outlaw the use of the bomb except in retaliation is the only cause of the absence of an agreement with the Soviet Union over atomic control. The Russians have made it clear that they will do everything in their power to prevent a supranational regime from coming into existence. They not only reject it in the range of atomic energy: they reject it sharply on principle, and thus have spurned in advance any overture to join a limited world government.

Mr. Gromyko [Soviet diplomat Andrei Gromyko] has rightly said that the essence of the American atomic proposal is that national sovereignty is not compatible with the atomic era. He declares that the Soviet Union cannot accept this thesis. The reasons he gives are obscure, for they quite obviously are pretexts. But what seems to be true is that the Soviet leaders believe they cannot preserve the social structure of the Soviet state in a supranational regime. The Soviet government is determined to maintain its present social structure, and the leaders of Russia, who hold their great power through the nature of that structure, will spare no effort to prevent a supranational regime from coming into existence, to control atomic energy or anything else.

The Russians may be partly right about the difficulty of retaining their present social structure in a supranational regime, though in time they may be brought to see that this is a far lesser loss than remaining isolated from a world of law. But at present they appear to be guided by their fears, and one must admit that the United States has made ample contributions to these fears, not only as to atomic energy but in many other respects. Indeed this country has conducted its Russian policy as though it were convinced that fear is the greatest of all diplomatic instruments.

That the Russians are striving to prevent the formation of a supranational security system is no reason why the rest of the world should not work to create one. It has been pointed out that the Russians have a way of resisting with all their arts what they do not wish to have happen; but once it happens, they can be flexible and accommodate themselves to it. So it would be well for the United States and other powers not to permit the Russians to veto an attempt to create supranational security. They can proceed with some hope that once the Russians see they cannot prevent such a regime they may join it.

Trust and Reassurance Are Needed

So far the United States has shown no interest in preserving the security of the Soviet Union. It has been interested in its own security, which is characteristic of the competition which marks the conflict for power between sovereign states. But one cannot know in advance what would be the effect on Russian fears if the American people forced their leaders to pursue a policy of substituting law for the present anarchy of international relations. In a world of law, Russian security would be equal to our own, and for the American people to espouse this wholeheartedly, something that should be possible under the workings of democracy, might work a kind of miracle in Russian thinking.

At present the Russians have no evidence to convince them that the American people are not contentedly supporting a policy of military preparedness which they regard as a policy of deliberate intimidation. If they had evidences of a passionate desire by Americans to preserve peace in the one way it can be maintained, by a supranational regime of law, this would upset Russian calculations about the peril to Russian security in current trends of American thought. Not until a genuine, convincing offer is made to the Soviet Union, backed by an aroused American public, will one be entitled to say what the Russian response would be.

It may be that the first response would be to reject the world of law. But if from that moment it began to be clear to the Russians that such a world was coming into existence without them, and that their own security was being increased, their ideas necessarily would change.

A New World Government

I am in favor of inviting the Russians to join a world government authorized to provide security, and if they are unwilling to join, to proceed to establish supranational security without them. Let me admit quickly that I see great peril in such a course. If it is adopted it must be done in a way to make it utterly clear that the new regime is not a combination of power against Russia. It must be a combination that by its composite nature will greatly reduce the chances of war. It will be more diverse in its interests than any single state, thus less likely to resort to aggressive or preventive war. It will be larger, hence stronger than any single nation. It will be geographically much more extensive, and thus more difficult to defeat by military means. It will be dedicated to supranational security, and thus escape the emphasis on national supremacy which is so strong a factor in war.

If a supranational regime is set up without Russia, its service to peace will depend on the skill and sincerity with which it is done. Emphasis should always be apparent on the desire to have Russia take part. It must be clear to Russia, and no less so to the nations comprising the organization, that no penalty is incurred or implied because a nation declines to join. If the Russians do not join at the outset, they must be sure of a welcome when they do decide to join. Those who create the organization must understand that they are building with the final objective of obtaining Russian adherence.

These are abstractions, and it is not easy to outline the specific lines a partial world government must follow to induce the Russians to join. But two conditions are clear to me: the new organization must have no military secrets; and the Russians must be free to have observers at every session of the organization, where its new laws are drafted, discussed, and adopted, and where its policies are decided. That would destroy the great factory of secrecy where so many of the world's suspicions are manufactured.

It may affront the military-minded person to suggest a regime that does not maintain any military secrets. He has been taught to believe that secrets thus divulged would enable a war-minded nation to seek to conquer the earth. (As to the so-called secret of the atomic bomb, I am assuming the Russians will have this through their own efforts within a short time.) I grant there is a risk in not maintaining military secrets. If a sufficient number of nations have pooled their strength they can take this risk, for their security will be greatly increased. And it can be done with greater assurance because of the decrease of fear, suspicion, and distrust that will result. The tensions of the increasing likelihood of war in a world based on sovereignty would be replaced by the relaxation of the growing confidence in peace. In time this might so allure the Russian people that their leaders would mellow in their attitude toward the West.

A New Philosophy Is Needed to Achieve Peace

John Paul II

A number of religious figures and groups had been outspoken opponents of nuclear weapons from the start of the Cold War. Within days of Truman's announcement of the atomic bombing in Hiroshima, several prominent American religious publications claimed that the use of the bomb against a civilian population had, as an editorial in the August 29, 1945, issue of the *Christian Century* put it, "placed our nation in an indefensible moral position." In March 1946 the Federal Council of Churches—a group of leading Protestant clergy and teachers—echoed this sentiment in a report that condemned the atomic bombings because their "moral cost was too high." Many Catholic leaders also took this position, including the editor of the Catholic weekly *Commonweal*, who wrote on August 24, 1945, that the "name Hiroshima, the name Nagasaki, are names for American guilt and shame."

While the dissent was not unanimous among theologians and clergy, the opposition among religious leaders to nuclear weapons and the arms race remained fairly consistent for the duration of the Cold War. As the Cold War intensified again in the early 1980s after a long period of relative calm, Pope John Paul II carried on this tradition by issuing an address to the General Assembly of the United Nations on June 7, 1982, in which he called the nuclear

John Paul II, address to the General Assembly of the United Nations, New York, June 7, 1982.

arms race—and the policy of mutual deterrence which was used to explain it—irrational and unethical. The pope called on the United States and the Soviet Union to step up their efforts at negotiating an end to the arms race and beginning the process of disarmament. This change was necessary not only to reduce the threat of nuclear war, he stated, but also to allow the world to focus on what he saw as a larger moral crisis, of which the arms race was merely a symptom. He argued that the opposing sides in the Cold War must abandon the notion that their individual ideologies were so worthy of defense that they justified the risk of nuclear war and focus instead on their shared moral responsibility to all humanity. Partly spurred by the pope's message, religious leaders around the world played a visible role in the nuclear disarmament and antiwar movements that flourished in the mid-1980s.

In June 1978, my Predecessor Pope Paul VI sent a personal message to the First Special Session of the United Nations devoted to Disarmament, in which he expressed his hopes that such an effort of good will and political wisdom by the international community would bring the result that humanity was looking for.

Four years later you are gathered here again to ask yourselves if those initiatives have been—at least partially—realized.

The answer to that question seems neither very reassuring nor very encouraging. If one compares the situation in the area of disarmament four years ago with that of today, there seems to be very little improvement. Some, in fact, think that there has been a deterioration at least in the sense that hopes born of that period could now be labeled as simple illusions. Such a stance could very easily lend itself to discouragement and impel those who are responsible to seek elsewhere for the solution to these problems—general or particular—which continue to disturb the lives of people.

That is, in fact, how many see the current situation. Figures from various sources all point to a serious increase in military expenditures represented by a greater production of different kinds of weapons along with which, according to specialized institutes, there is a new rise in the sale of weapons. Recently the news media has given a great deal of attention to research and use on a wider scale of chemical weapons. Moreover new kinds of nuclear weapons have also come into existence.

Before an assembly as competent as this one, there is no need to repeat the figures which your own organization has published on this subject. It is sufficient, as an indication, to refer to the study according to which the sum total of military expenditures on the planet corresponds to a mean of $100 per person per year, a figure which for many people who live on this earth is all they would have annually to survive. . . .

This is the voice of one who has no interests nor political power, nor even less military force. It is a voice which is heard here again in this hall thanks to your courtesy. Here where practically all the nations, great and small, of the world come together, my words are meant to be the echo of the moral conscience of humanity "in the pure sense," if you will grant me that expression. My words bear with them no special interests or concerns of a nature which could mar their witness value and make them less credible.

A conscience illumined and guided by Christian faith, without doubt, but which is by that fact nonetheless profoundly human. It is therefore a conscience which is shared by all men and women of sincerity and good will.

My voice is the echo of the concerns and aspirations, the hopes and the fears of millions of men and women who, from every walk of life, are looking toward this Assembly asking, as they hope, if there will come forth some reassuring light or if there will be a new and more worrisome disappointment. Without claiming a mandate from all these people, I believe I can make myself the faithful interpreter to you of the feelings which are theirs.

I neither wish nor am I able to enter into the technical and political aspects of the problem of disarmament as they stand before you today. However, I would like to call your attention to some ethical principles which are at the heart of every discussion and every decision that might be looked for in this field.

The World Needs Peace

My point of departure is rooted in a statement unanimously agreed upon not only by your citizens but also by the governments that you lead or you represent: the world wants peace; the world needs peace.

In our modern world to refuse peace means not only to provoke the sufferings and the loss that—today more than ever—war, even a limited one, implies: it could also involve the total destruction of entire regions, not to mention the threat of possible or probable catastrophes in ever vaster and possibly even universal proportions.

Those who are responsible for the life of peoples seem above all to be engaged in a frantic search for political means and technical solutions which would allow the results of eventual conflicts "to be contained." While having to recognize the limits of their efforts in this direction, they persist in believing that in the long run war is inevitable. Above all this is found in the specter of a possible military confrontation between the two major camps which divide the world today and continues to haunt the future of humanity.

Certainly no power, and no statesman, would be of a mind to admit to planning war or to wanting to take such an initiative. Mutual distrust, however, makes us believe or fear that because others might nourish designs or desires of this type, each, especially among the great powers, seems to envisage no other possible solution than through necessity to prepare sufficiently strong defense to be able to respond to an eventual attack.

Deterrence Is a Failed Philosophy

Many even think that such preparations constitute the way—even the only way—to safeguard peace in some fashion or at least to impede to the utmost in an efficacious way the outbreak of wars, especially major conflicts which might lead to the ultimate holocaust of humanity and the destruction of the civilization that man has constructed so laboriously over the centuries.

In this approach one can see the "philosophy of peace" which was proclaimed in the ancient Roman principle: *Si vis pacem, para bellum* [roughly, "If you seek peace prepare for

Soviet women from Khabarovsk protest in June 1984, demon-strating their support for actions to preserve peace in the world.

war"]. Put in modern terms, this "philosophy" has the label of "deterrence," and one can find it in various guises of the search for a "balance of forces" which sometimes has been called, and not without reason, the "balance of terror."

As my Predecessor Paul VI put it: "The logic underlying the request for the balances of power impels each of the adversaries to seek to ensure a certain margin of superiority, for fear of being left at a disadvantage."

Thus in practice the temptation is easy—and the danger always present—to see the search for balance turned into a search for superiority of a type that sets off the arms race in an even more dangerous way. . . .

Perhaps no other question of our day touches so many aspects of the human condition as that of armaments and disarmament. There are questions on the scientific and technical level; there are social and economic questions. There are deep problems of a political nature that touch the relations between states and among peoples.

The Catholic View of the Arms Race

Our world-wide arms systems impinge in great measure on cultural developments. But at the heart of them all there are present spiritual questions which concern the very identity of man, and his choices for the future and for generations yet to come. Sharing my thoughts with you, I am conscious of all the technical, scientific, social, economic, political aspects, but especially of the ethical, cultural and spiritual ones.

Since the end of the Second World War and the beginning of the "atomic age," the attitude of the Holy See and the Catholic Church has been clear. The Church has continually sought to contribute to peace and to build a world that would not have recourse to war to solve disputes. It has encouraged the maintenance of an international climate of mutual trust and cooperation. It has supported those structures which would help ensure peace. It has called attention to the disastrous effects of war. With the growth of new and more lethal means of destruction, it has pointed to the dangers involved and, going beyond the immediate perils, it has indicated what values to develop in order to foster cooperation, mutual trust, fraternity and peace.

My Predecessor, Pius XII, as early as 1946, referred to "the might of new instruments of destruction" which "brought the problems of disarmament into the center of international discussions under completely new aspects."

Each successive Pope and the Second Vatican Council [a lengthy series of meetings from 1962–1965 in which the Church's position on contemporary affairs was debated] continued to express their convictions, introducing them into the changing and developing situation of armaments and arms control. If men would bend to the task with good will and with the goal of peace in their hearts and in their plans, then adequate measures could be found, appropriate structures erected to ensure the legitimate security of every people in mutual respect and peace; thus the need for these grand arsenals of fear and the threat of death would become superfluous.

The teaching of the Catholic Church in this area has been clear and consistent. It has deplored the arms race, called nonetheless for mutual progressive and verifiable reduction of armaments as well as greater safeguards against possible misuse of these weapons. It has done so while urging that the independence, freedom and legitimate security of each and every nation be respected.

I wish to reassure you that the constant concern and consistent efforts of the Catholic Church will not cease until there is a general verifiable disarmament, until the hearts of all are won over to those ethical choices which will guarantee a lasting peace.

The Need for Respectful Negotiation

In turning to the current debate that concerns you, and to the subject at hand, we must recognize that no element in international affairs stands alone and isolated from the many-faceted interests of nations. However, it is one thing to recognize the interdependence of questions; it is another to exploit them in order to gain advantage in another. Armaments, nuclear weapons and disarmament are too important in themselves and for the world ever to be made part of a strategy which would exploit their intrinsic importance in favor of politics or other interests.

Therefore, it is important and right that every serious proposal that would contribute to real disarmament and that would create a better climate be given the prudent and objective consideration it deserves. Even small steps can have a value which would go beyond their material or technical aspects. Whatever the area under consideration, we need today freshness of perspective and a capacity to listen respectfully and carefully to the honest suggestions of every responsible party in this matter.

In this context there is what I would call the phenomenon of rhetoric. In an area already tense and fraught with unavoidable dangers, there is no place for exaggerated speech or threatening stances. Indulgence in rhetoric, in inflamed and impassioned vocabulary, in veiled threat and scare tactics can only exacerbate a problem that needs sober and diligent examination.

Peace Movements Are Developing

On the other hand, governments and their leaders cannot carry on the affairs of state independent of the wishes of their peoples. The history of civilization gives us stark examples of what happens when that is tried. Currently the fear and preoccupation of so many groups in various parts of the world reveal that people are more and more frightened about what would happen if irresponsible parties unleash some nuclear war.

In fact, just about everywhere peace movements have been developing. In several countries, these movements, which have become very popular, are being supported by an increasing sector of the citizenry from various social levels, different age groups and backgrounds, but especially by youth. The ideological bases of these movements are multiple. Their projects, proposals and policies vary greatly and can often lend themselves to political exploitation. However, all these differences of form and shape manifest a profound and sincere desire for peace. . . .

In current conditions "deterrence" based on balance, certainly not as an end in itself but as a step on the way toward a progressive disarmament, may still be judged morally acceptable. Nonetheless in order to ensure peace, it is indispensable not to be satisfied with this minimum which is always susceptible to the real danger of explosion.

A Complete Program of Disarmament

What then can be done? In the absence of a supranational authority of the type Pope John XXIII sought in his Encyclical Pacem in terris, one which one would have hoped to find in the United Nations Organization, the only realistic response to the threat of war still is negotiation. Here I would like to remind you of an expression of Saint Augustine which I have already cited in another context: "Destroy war by the words of negotiations, but do not destroy men by the sword." Today once again, before you all, I reaffirm my confidence in the power of true negotiations to arrive at just and equitable solutions. Such negotiations demand patience and diligence and most notably lead to a reduction of armaments that is balanced, simultaneous and internationally controlled.

To be even more precise: the development of armaments seems to lead to the increasing interdependence of kinds of armaments. In these conditions, how can one countenance a balanced reduction if negotiations do not include the whole gamut of arms? To that end the continuation of the study of the "Complete Program of Disarmament" that your organization has already undertaken, could facilitate the needed coordination of different forums and bring to their results greater truth, equity and efficacy. . . .

The Relationship Between Disarmament and Development

In his address to the United Nations Organization on October 4, 1965, Pope Paul VI stated a profound truth when he said: "Peace, as you know, is not built up only by means of politics or the balance of forces and interests. It is constructed with the mind, with ideas, with works of peace." The products of the mind—ideas—the products of culture, and the creative forces of peoples are meant to be shared. Strategies of peace which remain on the scientific and technical level and which merely measure out balances and verify controls will never be sufficient for real peace unless bonds that link peoples to one another are forged and strengthened. Build up the links that unite people together. Build up the means that will enable peoples and nations to share their culture and values with one another. Put aside all the narrow interests that leave one nation at the mercy of another economically, socially or politically.

In this same vein, the work of many qualified experts plumbing the relationship between disarmament and development is to be commended for study and action. The prospect of diverting material and resources from the development of arms to the development of peoples is not a new one. Nonetheless, it is a pressing and compelling one which the Catholic Church has for a long time endorsed. Any new dynamism in that direction coming from this Assembly would be met with the approbation and support of men and women of good will everywhere.

The building of links among peoples means the rediscovery and reassertion of all the values that reinforce peace and that join people together in harmony. This also means the renewal of what is best in the heart of man, the heart that seeks the good of the other in friendship and love.

The Arms Race Is a Symptom of a Larger Problem

May I close with one last consideration. The production and the possession of armaments are a consequence of an ethical crisis that is disrupting society in all its political, social and economic dimensions. Peace, as I have already said several times, is the result of respect for ethical principles. True disarmament, that which will actually guarantee peace among peoples, will come about only with the resolution of this ethical crisis. To the extent that the efforts at arms reduction and then of total disarmament are not matched by parallel ethical renewal, they are doomed in advance to failure.

The attempt must be made to put our world aright and to eliminate the spiritual confusion born from a narrow-minded search for interest or privilege or by the defense of ideological claims: this is a task of first priority if we wish to measure any progress in the struggle for disarmament. Otherwise we are condemned to remain at face-saving activities.

For the root cause of our insecurity can be found in this profound crisis of humanity. By means of creating consciences sensitive to the absurdity of war, we advance the value of creating the material and spiritual conditions which will lessen the glaring inequalities and which will restore to everyone that minimum of space that is needed for the freedom of the spirit.

The great disparity between the rich and the poor living together on this one planet is no longer supportable in a world of rapid universal communications, without giving birth to a justified resentment that can turn to violence. Moreover the spirit has basic and inalienable rights. For it is with justice that these rights are demanded in countries where the space is denied them to live in tranquillity according to their own convictions. I invite all those struggling for peace to commit themselves to the effort to eliminate the true causes of the insecurity of man of which the terrible arms race is only one effect.

What Should Be Done?

To reverse the current trend in the arms race involves, therefore, a parallel struggle on two fronts: on the one side, an immediate and urgent struggle by governments to reduce progressively and equally their armaments; on the other hand, a more patient but nonetheless necessary struggle at the level of the consciences of peoples to take their responsibility in regard to the ethical cause of the insecurity that breeds violence by coming to grips with the material and spiritual inequalities of our world.

With no prejudice of any kind, let us unite all our intellectual and spiritual forces, those of statesmen, of citizens, of religious leaders, to put an end to violence and hatred and to seek out the paths of peace.

Peace is the supreme goal of the activity of the United Nations. It must become the goal of all men and women of good will. Unhappily still in our days, sad realities cast their shadows across the international horizon, causing the suffering of destruction, such that they could cause humanity to lose the hope of being able to master its own future in harmony and in the collaboration of peoples.

Despite the suffering that invades my soul, I feel empowered, even obliged, solemnly to reaffirm before all the world what my Predecessors and I myself have repeated so often in the name of conscience, in the name of morality, in the name of humanity and in the name of God:

Peace is not a utopia, nor an inaccessible ideal, nor an unrealizable dream.

War is not an inevitable calamity.

Peace is possible.

And because it is possible, peace is our duty: our grave duty, our supreme responsibility.

Certainly peace is difficult: certainly it demands much good will, wisdom, and tenacity. But man can and he must make the force of reason prevail over the reasons of force.

The Nuclear Freeze Movement

Helen Broinowski Caldicott

Helen Broinowski Caldicott is an Australian pediatrician who has also been a prominent activist since the early 1970s, especially for antinuclear causes. Her books *Nuclear Madness* (1979) and *Missile Envy* (1984) are among the most important works protesting the role of atomic energy and nuclear weapons in the Cold War world. During the early 1980s, she became one of the most visible icons of the "Nuclear Freeze" movement, a broad coalition of antinuclear organizations such as the Physicians for Social Responsibility (PSR) that sought to get both the United States and the Soviet Union to stop increasing the size of their nuclear arsenals. For these groups, a freeze was seen as a necessary and practical first step toward disarmament, and therefore a way to reduce the risk of nuclear war immediately.

This excerpt from Caldicott's autobiography describes some of her memories of the freeze movement, especially her participation in a rally held in New York's Central Park in the spring of 1982. Although crowd estimates vary somewhat (at minimum, three-quarters of a million people attended) the rally was the single largest antinuclear demonstration of the Cold War and served as a clear illustration that opposition to existing nuclear weapons policies was widespread among the American people. Though the formal legislation that Caldicott and her allies hoped for was never passed in Congress, the freeze movement did help

Helen Broinowski Caldicott, *A Desperate Passion: An Autobiography.* New York: W.W. Norton & Company, 1996. Copyright © 1996 by Helen Broinowski Caldicott. Reproduced by permission.

keep the national debate over nuclear weapons going during a time of renewed U.S.-Soviet tensions. Within ten years of the Central Park rally, several nuclear arms reductions treaties had been signed that actually exceeded the original goals of the freeze movement and helped to lessen the overwhelming anxiety that Caldicott cites in the introduction to her autobiography as her main reason for getting involved with antinuclear activism.

I was standing with the PSR [Physicians for Social Responsibility] contingent in a New York street on a crisp, sparkling June day when it suddenly dawned on me that I would never make it to the podium on time. It was 12 June 1982, the day that 1 million people crowded the streets of New York to protest the continuing dangers of the nuclear arms race during the United Nations' second special session on disarmament.

I was scheduled to speak at 12:45, and it was already 12:15. I fled through streets packed with every imaginable contingent, from Black Lesbians for Peace to the Church of Christ, the Mormons, Southern Baptists, and Grandmothers for Peace. Never had the city witnessed such a huge crowd—all had come to bear witness to the monumental wickedness of the nuclear arms race.

I arrived backstage in Central Park distressed and short of breath with five minutes to spare. As I stood and watched [actor] Orson Welles being winched onto the stage in his wheelchair because of his massive size, I tried to imagine just what I would say in three minutes to this ocean of faces to focus their attention upon the dire probabilities if we continued to countenance the actions of the nuclear nations.

Orson gave a passionate speech about the gravity of the situation, and then it was my turn. "Let me tell you what would happen if a nuclear bomb were dropped on Central Park," I began. My voice was surprisingly confident, and I took courage: after all, I had said similar things before, all over the country. "The bomb will come in on a missile travelling at about twenty times the speed of sound, moving on a ballistic trajectory. If it explodes at ground level on a clear day like today, it will release heat equivalent to that of the sun—several million degrees Celsius—in a fraction of a second. It will dig a hole three-quarters of a mile wide and eight hundred feet deep, converting all the people, buildings, and earth and rocks below to radioactive fallout particles which will be shot up into the atmosphere in a mushroom cloud.

"Because the human body is composed mostly of water, it turns into gas when it is exposed to thousands of degrees Celsius. When the atomic bomb dropped on Hiroshima on 6 August 1945, a little boy was reaching up to catch a red dragonfly. There was a blinding flash, and he disappeared, leaving only the shadow of his body on the pavement behind him.

"Anyone who watches the flash without being vaporised will have his or her eyes melted by the intense heat . . . other people will be turned into charcoal. In a book called *Unforgettable Fire* [published in 1977 by Japan Broadcasting Corporation] Hiroshima survivors drew pictures of scenes they remembered. One depicted a mother holding her baby, standing on one foot, running; she and the infant had been turned into a charcoal statue."

I ended by quoting Richard Nixon, who said: "Don't listen to what we say, watch what we do," reminding the audience how horribly dangerous this was when applied to the [Ronald] Reagan administration. This became the quote of the week in the *New York Times*. When I finished, there was an eerie silence. Then wave after wave of applause broke over me. It felt wonderful to move so many people, knowing that the antinuclear movement had grown so fast. That was one of the most exciting moments of my life. I walked off the stage feeling that the power of the people was immutable and would save the earth.

The Immediate Reaction to the March

As I left the park, a young woman came racing up to me and asked, "Are you Helen Caldicott?"

"I am."

"I was in the shower the other day and heard a voice on television say that every town and city with a population of 25,000 people or more in the United States is targeted with at least one bomb. I didn't know that, that's why I'm here." I'm sure that many thousands were there that day because of the enormous power wielded by the media to educate and influence people's thinking. Pat Kingsley, who had so facilitated my presence in the media, had helped to pack Central Park.

The *New York Times* devoted a lot of space to reporting the march as a local city event, saying that amazingly there was no rubbish left to clean up in the wake of 1 million people; it had been entirely peaceful. But at no point did the paper ever examine the issues that had created the largest political gathering in the history of the country, allotting only one small editorial to a discussion of the nuclear freeze movement. And it was dismissive to the point of arrogance, saying that judging by the march and rally, the freeze was supported by a vast spectrum of American citizens, from grandmothers to church groups to children, and that such support was unique in the history of the United States—but that the desired change was not feasible.

I couldn't believe this. Not feasible? When a million people were demanding a bilateral end to the nuclear arms race? When we were asking the USA and USSR to stop testing, developing, producing, and deploying all nuclear weapons and delivery systems? Of course it was feasible, as well as simple and fair. The trouble was that we were up against the architects of the nuclear arms race, who greatly influenced the thinking of the press, [states]men such as Henry Kissinger, Eugene Rostow, Fred Ikle, James Schlesinger, and the two Richards—Perle and Burt—among others, members of the old boys' club, and they were almost offended by an idea that had emanated from the very foundation of American society.

Nevertheless, the events of the 12th of June 1982 showed that the antinuclear movement was now a force to be reckoned with. And some members of the old boys' club did actually support us, including William Colby, the former chief of the CIA and Paul Warnke, ambassador to the SALT [Strategic Arms Limitation Talks] II negotiations. Soon after the march, not to be outdone, the military-industrial complex, clearly intimidated by the show of popular pressure against it, retaliated and called for a major new engineering initiative in space known as Star Wars, which would move the concept of nuclear war into space.

Nuclear Freeze Politics

Reagan responded to the march in a derogatory fashion: you could get as many people at a rock concert. But he then began hijacking the language we used: "Nuclear war must never be fought and can never be won," he said. We were winning, yet not winning. The momentum of the movement was not to be stopped, though. In February 1982 Senators Ted Kennedy and Mark Hatfield had introduced a freeze resolution in the Senate, supported by 17 other senators; the House version of the resolution had 122 cosponsors. In the same month [Soviet premier] Leonid Brezhnev urged a resumption of talks on limiting strategic arms, suggesting an interim freeze on the deployment of long-range Cruise missiles, and a *Los Angeles Times*/CNN poll showed that Americans would support a freeze by a margin of 3-2 if the question was put on local ballots.

On 18 May, in reply to a Reagan proposal for informal talks aimed at reducing U.S.-USSR arsenals of nuclear warheads by one-third, Brezhnev proposed that the freeze should go into effect as soon as the talks began. On 29 June, seventeen days after the march and nine days before the talks began in Geneva, a national mayors' conference adopted a resolution calling on President Reagan to begin talks with the Soviets on a mutual, verifiable freeze. But a month later Reagan aborted talks with Great Britain and the USSR on a comprehensive ban on nuclear testing, which had been in abeyance since 1980, saying he doubted that such a ban could be verified and that new weapons needed to be tested. He followed this up with a letter to House speaker Tip O'Neill urging Congress to kill any freeze resolution. Nevertheless, on 28 July Congress approved a measure proposed by Congressman Les Aspin to bar funds for developing, testing, procuring, or operating any nuclear weapon that would undercut the SALT I or II treaty except in cases of "supreme national interest."

The freeze resolution, sponsored by Congressman Ed Markey from Massachusetts, was to come up in Congress on

5 August—the day before the anniversary of Hiroshima. It was a conscience vote, not legally binding (called a sense of the Congress), but the fact that the freeze was being debated in the Congress was an enormous step forward for us. . . .

On the evening of the 5th of August Ed [Markey] and I kept in close touch as the vote proceeded. He finally called me late at night almost in tears. By a margin of only two votes—204 to 202—the House had rejected the call for an immediate freeze, approving Reagan's phony option, a resolution to reduce arms. But the groundswell support for a freeze kept mounting, to the point where in November Reagan asserted that "foreign agents" were helping to instigate the movement, and that majority backers were sincere but misguided. The National Conference of State Legislatures did not agree with him, voting on the 10th of December to support the freeze resolution by 29 votes to 8.

By 1983 newspaper polls showed that 80 percent of the American public believed that nuclear war would not remain limited, be won, or be survived, and 77 percent believed that nuclear weapons policy was too important to be left in the hands of the experts alone. This was clearly a revolution in the public's thinking on the issue.

The antinuclear education program was gaining ground. By the end of 1982 PSR membership was up to 30,000, with 153 chapters in 48 states. Our symposia had covered more than 40 cities, with total attendances of more than 40,000. As well, PSR had also developed a model curriculum on the medical consequences of nuclear war for medical schools; and 124 schools had included it in their courses.

Nuclear Winter Makes War Even More Deadly

Carl Sagan and Richard Turco

Even as the nuclear stockpiles of both superpowers numbered in the tens of thousands, there were still some strategists who believed that a nuclear war could be "won." These people believed that a country could survive a nuclear war relatively intact with the right combination of advance preparation and defense, despite the dangers posed not only by nuclear explosions themselves but also the radioactive fallout that resulted from them. By the early 1980s, though, a group of scientists who called themselves TTAPS (the acronym was taken from their last names) developed the theory of "nuclear winter," which sharply contradicted any remaining sense that large-scale nuclear war was survivable.

Carl Sagan, David Duncan Professor of Astronomy and Space Sciences at the time of his death in 1996, and Richard Turco, professor of atmospheric science at the University of California at Los Angeles, were two of the five TTAPS scientists. Due to his immense public popularity—thanks largely to *Cosmos*, his public television series on astronomy—and his network of government connections associated with his work at NASA, Sagan was the one person most responsible for bringing the concept of nuclear winter into the public's consciousness through a series of television appearances, speaking engagements, and even congressional testimonies on the subject from 1983 to 1986. In this excerpt from Sagan's and Turco's 1990 book *A Path Where No Man Thought*, the two scientists lay out the basics behind the theory. They argue that the long-term survival of nuclear war is made nearly impossible because of the smoke and dust that would collect in the atmosphere after even a fairly limited nuclear war. This material is not only immediately dangerous because it is radioactive; it would also block out enough of the light coming from the sun to lower the earth's temperature to a point that the planet could no longer sustain life.

The nuclear winter hypothesis proved to be extremely persuasive in contradicting any remaining belief that nuclear war could actually be fought and won. It helped to rally popular dissent in the United States against the continuation of the arms race and, in doing so, helped to bring about some of the arms reduction treaties that were signed during the final years of the Cold War.

Life on Earth is exquisitely dependent on the climate. The average surface temperature of the Earth—averaged, that is, over day and night, over the seasons, over latitude, over land and ocean, over coastline and continental interior, over mountain range and desert—is about 13°C, 13 Centigrade degrees above the temperature at which fresh water freezes. (The corresponding temperature on the Fahrenheit scale is 55°F.) It's harder to change the temperature of the oceans than of the continents, which is why ocean temperatures are much more steadfast over the diurnal [daily] and seasonal cycles than are the temperatures in the middle of large continents. Any global temperature change implies much larger local temperature changes, if you don't live near the ocean.

A prolonged global temperature drop of a few degrees C would be a disaster for agriculture; by 10°C, whole ecosystems would be imperiled; and by 20°C, almost all life on Earth would be at risk. The margin of safety is thin.

It is a central fact of our existence that the Earth would be some 35°C colder than it is today if the global temperature were to depend only on how much sunlight is absorbed by the Earth. This is a calculation routinely performed in introductory astronomy and climatology courses: You consider the intensity of sunlight reaching the top of the atmosphere, subtract the fraction of sunlight that's reflected back to space, and let the remainder—which is mainly absorbed by the Earth's surface—account for our planet's temperature. You balance the amount of radiation heating the Earth with the amount that is radiated (not reflected) by the Earth back to space. The temperature you derive is, disturbingly, some 35°C colder than the actual surface temperature of the Earth. If this were all there were to the physics, the average temperature of the Earth would be below the freezing point of water; the oceans, still kilometers thick, would be made of ice; and almost all familiar forms of life—ourselves included—would never have come to be.

The missing factor, what we have ignored in this simple calculation, is the increasingly well-known "greenhouse" effect. Gases in the Earth's atmosphere, mainly water vapor and carbon dioxide, are transparent to ordinary visible sunlight but opaque to the infrared radiation that the Earth radiates to space as it attempts to cool itself off. These greenhouse gases act as a kind of blanket, warming the Earth just enough to make the clement and agreeable world we are privileged to inhabit today. Were the greenhouse effect to be significantly meddled with—turned up or down, much less turned off—it would constitute a planetwide disaster. This is in part what nuclear winter is about.

Nuclear War and the Atmosphere

In a nuclear war, powerful nuclear explosions at the ground would propel fine particles high into the stratosphere. Much of the dust would be carried up by the fireball itself. Some would be sucked up the stem of the mushroom cloud. Even much more modest explosions on or above cities would produce massive fires, as occurred in Hiroshima and Nagasaki. These fires consume wood, petroleum, plastics, roofing tar, natural gas, and a wide variety of other combustibles. The resulting smoke is far more dangerous to the climate than is the dust. Two kinds of smoke are generated. Smoldering combustion is a low-temperature, flameless burning in which fine, oily, bluish-white organic particles are produced. Cigarette smoke is an example. By contrast, in flaming combustion—when there's an adequate supply of oxygen—the burning organic material is converted in significant part to elemental carbon, and the sooty smoke is very dark. Soot is one of the blackest materials nature is able to manufacture. As in an oil refinery fire, or a burning pile of auto tires, or a conflagration in a modern skyscraper—more generally, in any big city fire—great clouds of roiling, ugly, dark, sooty smoke would rise high above the cities in a nuclear war, and spread first in longitude, then in latitude.

The high-altitude dust particles reflect additional sunlight back to space and cool the Earth a little. More important are the dense palls of black smoke high in the atmosphere; they block the sunlight from reaching the lower atmosphere, where the greenhouse gases mainly reside. These gases are thereby deprived of their leverage on the global climate. The greenhouse effect is turned down and the Earth's surface is cooled much more.

Because cities and petroleum repositories are so rich in combustible materials, it doesn't require very many nuclear explosions over them to make so much smoke as to obscure the entire Northern Hemisphere and more. If the dark, sooty clouds are nearly opaque and cover an extensive area, then the greenhouse effect can be almost entirely turned off. In the more likely case that some sunlight trickles through, the temperatures nevertheless may drop 10 or 20°C or more, depending on season and geographical locale. In many places, it may at midday get as dark as it used to be on a moonlit night before the nuclear war began. The resulting environmental changes may last for months or years.

If the greenhouse effect is a blanket in which we wrap ourselves to keep warm, nuclear winter kicks the blanket off. This darkening and cooling of the Earth following nuclear war—along with other ancillary consequences—is what we mean by nuclear winter.

A typical temperature for a point on the *land* surface of the Earth, averaged over latitude, season, and time of day, is roughly 15°C (59°F). If there were no greenhouse effect whatever, the corresponding temperature would be about –20°C (–4°F). The difference between the planetary environment with the greenhouse effect and without it is the difference between clement conditions and deep freeze. Tampering with the greenhouse effect—especially in ways that reduce it—can be very risky. . . .

If we were to double the present concentration of the greenhouse gas carbon dioxide in the Earth's atmosphere—as will happen in a few decades if present trends continue—the surface temperature will likely increase by a few degrees. Following a major volcanic explosion the temperature can *de*crease by as much as a few degrees. During an Ice Age, the global temperatures are a few degrees colder yet, approaching the freezing point of water. And in a nuclear winter, depending on severity, the temperatures can become still colder, ranging well below freezing. Just how cold it gets depends on many variables, including how the nuclear war is "fought." But even the middle range of these nuclear winter effects represents the severest climatic catastrophe ever to have occurred during the tenure of humans on this planet. Even in the range of temperature overlap, a mild nuclear winter is harsher than a severe Ice Age, because of its rapid onset (weeks rather than centuries or millennia)—although its duration is much briefer.

The Origins and Potential Use of the Theory

The prediction of nuclear winter is drawn not, of course, from any direct experience with the consequences of global nuclear war, but rather from an investigation of the governing physics. (The problem does not lend itself to full experimental verification—at least not more than once.) The models derived are calibrated and tested by studies of the ambient climate of the Earth and other planets, and by observed climatic perturbations caused by volcanic explosions, massive forest fires, and great dust storms. Because scientific analyses of nuclear winter have now pretty well converged on a generally accepted set of predictions, and because nuclear winter holds implications for policy issues now undergoing urgent rethinking, we believe an updating and reconsideration of both science and policy is timely.

Conventional wisdom, no matter how deeply felt, may not be a reliable guide in an age of apocalyptic weapons. A number of studies have addressed the strategic and policy implications of nuclear winter. If the climatic consequences of nuclear war are serious, many have concluded that major changes in strategy, policy and doctrine may be required. . . . Nuclear winter has strong implications—in some cases primary, in many others at least reinforcing—for nearly every area of nuclear strategy, doctrine, policy, systems, deployment, and ethics. This broad impact stems from two basic and connected facts about nuclear winter: (a) its occurrence would present an unacceptable peril for the global civilization and for at least most of the human species; and (b) it puts at risk in the devastating aftermath of nuclear war not only survivors in the combatant nations, but also enormous numbers in noncombatant and far-distant nations—people, most of them, wholly uninvolved with whatever quarrel or fear precipitated the war.

Since we have not yet had a global nuclear war, our conclusions must remain inferential and therefore necessarily incomplete. Some counsel that policy should not be decided on the basis of incomplete information. But policy is *always* decided on incomplete information. Nuclear winter has now attained standards of completeness and accuracy at least comparable to those on which many vital real world policy decisions are made.

1939

January: Nuclear fission, the process from which atomic energy is derived, is discovered.

October: Albert Einstein writes a letter to President Franklin Roosevelt warning him that Nazi Germany might be attempting to build a nuclear bomb.

1941

December 7: The United States enters World War II after the Japanese attack on Pearl Harbor.

1942

September 23: The Manhattan Project, directed by J. Robert Oppenheimer, begins secretly developing an atomic bomb for the United States.

Fall: The secret Soviet atomic bomb project directed by Igor Kurchatov begins.

1945

April 12: Roosevelt dies, and Harry Truman becomes president.

July 16: The Trinity test at Alamogordo, New Mexico, marks the first successful atomic bomb explosion.

August 6 and 9: The United States explodes atomic bombs over Hiroshima and Nagasaki, respectively.

August 14: Japan surrenders, ending World War II.

1946

March 5: Former British prime minister Winston Churchill gives his Iron Curtain speech in Fulton, Missouri.

July: The Operation Crossroads nuclear tests are conducted by the United States at Bikini atoll in the South Pacific.

1948

June: Soviet troops blockade the western portion of Berlin. British and American planes begin airlifting supplies to the city soon thereafter.

1949

July: The North Atlantic Treaty Organization (NATO) is established among the United States and its allies.

August 29: The Soviet Union tests its first atomic bomb near Semipalatinsk, Kazakhstan.

1950

February: Senator Joseph McCarthy of Wisconsin publicly claims to have a list of "known Communists" working in the State Department.

March: National Security Council Resolution 68 (NSC 68) recommends a nuclear arsenal buildup and an aggressive military containment policy toward communism.

June: The Korean War begins.

1952

November 1: The United States detonates its first hydrogen bomb at Elugelab atoll.

1953

March 5: Joseph Stalin dies; after a power struggle of several months, Nikita Khrushchev succeeds him as premier.

June 19: Julius and Ethel Rosenberg are executed as Soviet nuclear spies.

July 27: The Korean War ends.

August 14: The Soviet Union successfully tests its first hydrogen bomb.

1955

May 14: The Warsaw Pact military alliance is formed among the Soviet Union and its allies in Eastern Europe.

1957

October 4: The Soviet Union launches *Sputnik*, the first artificial satellite. Both the Soviet Union and the United States successfully test intercontinental ballistic missiles (ICBMs) before the year is over.

1959

January: Communists led by Fidel Castro revolt successfully in Cuba.

July and September: Vice President Richard Nixon visits the Soviet Union, and Khrushchev visits the United States.

1960

May: An American U-2 spy plane is shot down over the Soviet Union; pilot Gary Francis Powers is eventually convicted of spying.

1961

April: The U.S.-sponsored Bay of Pigs invasion fails in Cuba.

August: The Berlin Wall is erected by the Soviets.

1962

October: The Cuban Missile Crisis takes place, during which the U.S. military goes on its highest state of nuclear alert for the only time in history.

1963

June 20: A "hot line" between the Kremlin and the White House is established.

August 5: The Limited Test-Ban Treaty is signed.

November 22: John F. Kennedy is assassinated, and Lyndon Johnson becomes president.

1964

October 15: Khrushchev is ousted and replaced by Leonid Brezhnev as Soviet premier.

1965

July: The first U.S. combat troops arrive in Vietnam.

December 28: China successfully tests its first hydrogen bomb.

1968

July: The Nuclear Arms Nonproliferation Treaty is signed.

1969

March: The Strategic Arms Limitation Talks (SALT) begin in Geneva.

1972

May: President Richard Nixon and Premier Brezhnev sign the Anti–Ballistic Missile (ABM) Treaty and the SALT I agreement.

1973

January 27: The Paris Accords establish a cease-fire in Vietnam; the last American combat troops leave Vietnam within two months.

1975

April 30: Saigon falls to Communist forces, and the United States evacuates its embassy there.

July 17: U.S. astronauts and Soviet cosmonauts cooperate in the Apollo-Soyuz linkage in outer space.

August 1: The Helsinki Accords are signed, recognizing official boundaries of several Eastern European nations in exchange for promises from the Soviets to improve human rights.

1979

June 18: The SALT II agreement is signed by U.S. president Jimmy Carter and Soviet premier Brezhnev.

December: The Soviet Union invades Afghanistan.

1980

July: The United States and many of its allies boycott the Moscow Summer Olympics in protest of the Soviet invasion of Afghanistan.

1983

March 23: President Ronald Reagan announces the Strategic Defense Initiative (SDI, or "Star Wars") program.

September 1: Korean Air Lines Flight 007 is shot down by a Soviet fighter jet.

1986

Soviet premier Mikhail Gorbachev announces glasnost ("openness") and perestroika ("restructuring") reform policies.

1987

December 8: Reagan and Gorbachev hold a summit meeting in Washington at which they sign the Intermediate-range Nuclear Forces (INF) Treaty.

1989

January: Soviet troops withdraw entirely from Afghanistan.

Summer: Numerous East European nations renounce their ties to the Soviet Union, and replace their Communist governments with democratic ones.

November 9: The Berlin Wall is torn down.

December: Gorbachev and President George H.W. Bush meet in Malta and declare the Cold War "officially over."

1990

Republics begin breaking away from the Soviet Union.

July: The London Declaration by NATO declares an end to the Cold War.

1991

July 31: The Strategic Arms Reduction Treaty (START) is signed by Bush and Gorbachev.

December 25: Gorbachev resigns as head of state.

December 31: The Soviet Union is dissolved.

FOR FURTHER RESEARCH

Books

Gar Alperovitz, *The Decision to Use the Atomic Bomb*. New York: Vintage, 1996.

Paul Boyer, *By the Bomb's Early Light: American Thought and Culture at the Dawn of the Atomic Age*. New York: Pantheon, 1985.

H.W. Brands, *The Devil We Knew: Americans and the Cold War*. New York: Oxford University Press, 1993.

Helen Caldicott, *Nuclear Madness: What You Can Do*. New York: W.W. Norton, 1994.

Freeman Dyson, *Weapons and Hope*. New York: Harper & Row, 1983.

Tom Engelhardt, *The End of Victory Culture: Cold War America and the Disillusioning of a Generation*. New York: BasicBooks, 1995.

Richard L. Garwin and Georges Charpak, *Megawatts and Megatons: A Turning Point in the Nuclear Age*. New York: Knopf, 2001.

Samuel Glasstone and Phillip J. Dolan, *The Effects of Nuclear Weapons*. Washington, DC: U.S. Government Printing Office, 1977.

John Hersey, *Hiroshima*. New York: Knopf, 1946.

Beatrice Heuser, *The Bomb: Nuclear Weapons in Their Historical, Strategic, and Ethical Context*. New York: Longman, 1999.

Fred Inglis, *The Cruel Peace: Everyday Life and the Cold War.* New York: BasicBooks, 1991.

Jeremy Isaacs and Taylor Downing, *Cold War: An Illustrated History, 1945–1991.* Boston: Little, Brown, 1998.

Herman Kahn, *Thinking About the Unthinkable in the 1980s.* New York: Simon & Schuster, 1985.

Fred Kaplan, *Wizards of Armageddon.* New York: Simon & Schuster, 1984.

Robert Jay Lifton, *Death in Life: The Survivors of Hiroshima.* New York: Simon & Schuster, 1967.

Robert Jay Lifton and Greg Mitchell, *Hiroshima in America: Fifty Years of Denial.* New York: Putnam, 1995.

J. Robert Oppenheimer, *The Open Mind.* New York: Simon & Schuster, 1955.

Richard Rhodes, *The Making of the Atomic Bomb.* New York: Simon & Schuster, 1986.

Kenneth D. Rose, *One Nation Underground: The Fallout Shelter in American Culture.* New York: New York University Press, 2001.

Jonathan Schell, *The Fate of the Earth.* New York: Knopf, 1982.

Ferenc Morton Szasz, *The Day the Sun Rose Twice: The Story of the Trinity Site Nuclear Explosion, July 16, 1945.* Albuquerque: University of New Mexico Press, 1995.

A. Costandina Titus, *Bombs in the Backyard: Atomic Testing and American Politics.* Reno: University of Nevada Press, 2001.

Tom Vanderbilt, *Survival City: Adventures Among the Ruins of Atomic America.* Princeton, NJ: Princeton Architectural Press, 2002.

Spencer R. Weart, *Nuclear Fear: A History of Images.* Cambridge, MA: Harvard University Press, 1988.

Allan M. Winkler, *Life Under a Cloud: American Anxiety About the Atom.* New York: Oxford University Press, 1993.

Films

Atomic Café, dir. Jayne Loader, Kevin Rafferty, and Pierce Rafferty. Archives Project, 1982.

The Day After, dir. Nicholas Meyer. ABC Motion Pictures, 1983.

Dr. Strangelove, or How I Learned to Stop Worrying and Love the Bomb, dir. Stanley Kubrick. Columbia Pictures, 1964.

Fail-Safe, dir. Sidney Lumet. Columbia Pictures, 1964.

The Manchurian Candidate, dir. John Frankenheimer. United Artists, 1962.

On the Beach, dir. Stanley Kramer. United Artists, 1959.

Testament, dir. Lynne Littman. American Playhouse, 1983.

Web Sites

Bulletin of the Atomic Scientists, www.bullatomsci.org. Founded in December 1945, this is the definitive publication on issues related to nuclear energy and nuclear weapons. Though its articles deal with complex material, they are written for a nonspecialist audience.

The Bureau of Atomic Tourism, www.atomictourist.com. A partly tongue-in-cheek, partly serious site that examines several important locales related to nuclear weapons, from Tinian airfield, where the Hiroshima and Nagasaki bombers took off, to several museums dedicated to nuclear issues. The site gives some historical context for each of these locations as well as information about how to travel to them.

CNN Interactive—Cold War, www.cnn.com/SPECIALS/cold.war. The companion Web site to a hugely popular television documentary series. The site contains video clips of archival, footage, primary documents related to nuclear weapons and policies, and discussions of the cultural effects of the Cold War on ordinary Americans.

The Cold War Museum, www.coldwar.org. An online collection of a variety of materials related to the Cold War, from photographs and sound bites to excerpts from primary and secondary sources.

The National Security Archive at George Washington University, www.gwu.edu/~nsarchiv. An archives project that digitizes and makes available to the public declassified governmental documents relating to national security issues, especially documents produced during the Cold War. Features a searchable archive as well as several special collections on specific topics.

INDEX